# MEITEI CALENDAR

## *Rites and Rituals in Manipur*

Sanasam Amal Singh

Maulana Abul Kalam Azad Institute of Asian Studies, Kolkata

ANSHAH Anshah Publishing House

Rs. 395; US$ 20

ISBN: 978-81-8364-72-5

Published in 2010

*Meitei Calendar: Rites and Rituals in Manipur*



*Published by:*
**ANSHAH PUBLISHING HOUSE**
LG, Pankaj Central Market, I.P. Ext.,
Patparganj, Delhi-110092, Tel: 22235152, 9810522367
Br.Off. 4617/18, Ansari Road, Darya Ganj,
New Delhi-110002, Tel: 65946453

# Contents


1. Introduction 5
2. Naming of the Months 15
3. Sharoi Khangba 27
4. Yaosang (Holi) 37
5. Lai Keithel Kaba 41
6. Ancestor Worship of Moirang Clan 45
7. Kongba Leithong Phatpa 53
8. Cheiraoba 59
9. Ancestor-Worship of Khuman Clan 63
10. Ancestor-Worship of Khaba Nganba Clan 67
11. Ancestor-Worship of Ningthouja Clan 71
12. Pakhangba Chenghongba 75
13. Koorak Lamtaiba 83
14. The Role of Male and Female in the Ritual Process 87
15. Changing Trends in the Ritual Life of the Meiteis 97

*Appendices*

1. Incantation 109
2. Apoklon 111
3. Declaration of the Outgoing Cheithaba 112

4. Declaration of the Incoming Cheithaba 113
5. Meigi Tengtha 115
6. Sana Lamok 117
7. Anam Athou Laison 119
8. Naheirol 121
9. Ahonglon 122

*Index* 125

# 1
# Introduction

In every community, whether primitive or advanced, past or present, there had always been a series of rituals and ceremonies, the number of which may vary from community to community or from society to society. These rituals and ceremonies have been one of the most important and outstanding features in the social and religious life of man since time immemorial. Mankind has not been able to cope successfully with the devastating forces of nature and at the same time, in the hours of his misfortunes and calamities, he feels that some evil spirit has cast a hostile and destructive look at him. In his limitations and finiteness or utter helplessness to contain these forces and in his attempt to have communion with the deities, man has to take recourse to series of rites and rituals, prayers and worships to the deities, both benevolent and malevolent. Through these rites and prayers, he expects that the evil designs of malevolent spirits would be warded off and the benevolent divinities would bestow prosperity and happiness to the people and the country.

Though every community has its own system of rituals, a very distinctive feature of the traditional Meitei society of Manipur, which marks off from other societies is that it has a periodical series of rites and ceremonies based on ancient religious traditions concerning almost every month of the Meitei calendar year. We know in a general way from ancient Meitei texts and age-old traditions that some of these rites and ceremonies originated in pre-historic period while some others evolved or were introduced in historical times.

Since the Meiteis exist in a single group, the community has its own rites, rituals and ceremonial practices right from the beginning. According to these rites social functions are organised. These social functions are performed in the months circulating within a year. Meiteis have twelve different names of twelve months which are current in Manipur. Some of the names are derived from the religious functions of the Meiteis, while some others have their origin in the seasonal changes of nature along with the different duties performed in the different seasons. But, we find no month taking its name from the stars. The Meitei claimed to know when one year is completed and when another year begins through the sense of predictions.

Today the twelve Meitei calendar months begin from the month of Sajibu (March-April) and end with the month of Lamda (February-March) in order of precedence. But in the remote past, Lamda was the first month of the year rather than the reverse as at present. The public festival, in Manipur, falls into two broad groups: those of Hindu origin, and those traditionally Meitei.[1] These divisions are not absolute, for there is incidence of Hindu influence on the Meitei festivals and traditional customs have been incorporated into the Hindu festivals.

At present the Manipur calendar follows the lunar month consisting of 30 lunar days beginning on the day of the new moon. It has been adjusted with the solar year through the formulated Bengali calendar popularly known as P.M. Bagchi's Nutan Directory Panjika.[2] This Panjika is widely adopted by the

1. S.N. Parratt, *The Religion of Manipur*, pub. 1980. p. 48.
2. Census of India 1996 (Manipur) Vol. XXII, Fairs and Festivals Part VII-B, Manipur Civil Service pp. 4-6.

Manipuris and it has served as the authentic reference book of the Manipuri astrologers. Here, our work puts emphasis on both the Meitei (Hindu Manipuri) festivals and the festivals of Meitei origin i.e. the pre-Hindu festivals.

Though they exist as a single and dominant group they are also influenced by other ethnic groups like the Nagas and the Kuki chin groups. Inter-ethnic relationship is inevitable right from the formation of kingship system. In course of time the Meitei professing Vaishnavism and the Nagas and the Kukis converting to Christianity. The acceptance of a major world religion like Christianity was a major factor of social change in the tribal belt of Manipur. Though Hinduism had its roots in Manipur prior to 18th century, it was only during the time of Garib Niwas, an 18th century Meitei king, that mass proselytism of the natives forced itself into the fold of Rama cult. Ramanism, while in its teething stage, was overshadowed by Krishnaism under the Chaitanya school whose Bhakti cult, absence of caste rigidity and devotion through singing of sankirtan found a firm foundation to become the state religion in the Meitei Hindu society. The reason for the popularity of Chaitanya Vaishnavism may be attributed to sankirtan itself which, infused by the artistic genius of the

Meiteis, created an atmosphere where dance and music became the dominant element of their religion and life, providing an emotional outlet to the people. The Bishnupriyas is also the main community which got absorbed in the Meitei fold. They considered themselves as autocthones of Manipur and claimed themselves like many other communities, to be the first settlers, the Kshatriyas in the valley as worshippers of Vishnu. Later on the Meitei rulers defeated them and forced them to migrate to other area, but later on they returned and settled down once again in Bishnupur and adjoining areas. Historical traditions reveal that the Bishnupriyas are the people whose progenitors had been taken as prisoners and were kept in the Mayang Imphal area. Later on they scattered themselves in different parts of Manipur and settled down. Such community movements were rather unrestricted in the ancient days as long as one accepted to be under a Pana (The Bishnupriya community and its movements have also been causing quite a stir in the majority community of the Meities in recent times). The Meiteis have considered them to be the carriers of an inferior culture and there lies the contention. While the Meiteis considered them and called them as 'Kalisha Macha'. McClulloch refers to them as 'grass cutters'. Another interesting fact that needs consideration is whether it is wise and factually correct to accept them as the children or the descendants of the 120 Hindu families of different castes who were brought into the valley by Garibniwaj in the later part of the 18th century, as has been made out by Allen in 1905.[3]

## Review of Literature

The primary sources, particularly the 'Puya' (manuscripts in original Meitei scripts), have been extensively used in the preparation of this work. It may be relevant to point out in this context that a critical examination of the 'Puya' is crucial in understanding the historical society of early Manipur. There are many 'Puyas', which deal with the calendaric rituals in the Pre-Hindu Meitei society. 'Tharon', which literally means the Lore of the months, is an important manuscript. In this literature we are able to know how the Meitei explains the name of twelve months. Secondly, the Khunung Lichat Sajat manuscript gives the details of the rites and rituals that have to be performed by the Meiteis in a calendar year. At present the above two manuscripts are hardly available. It is very necessary at the moment to preserve and to

3. B.C. Allen, *Assam District Gazetter-Naga Hills and Manipur*. Vol. IX, Part-II, Calcutta, 1985. p. 14.

interpret in a very authentic way to prevent from plagiarism. Apart from these, some other primary sources are discussed below:

**Primary Sources**

1. Thawanmichak Khenchong: deals with 27 stars.
2. Khuntaron: deals with traditional reading of days, months, and years, through lunar system.
3. Ningthourol Tanyeiba: deals with time keeping institute and its system.
4. Kontharol: deals with offering of Konyal (Prices of gold & silver) to different places.
5. Subika Laisaba: deals with astrological work with illustrations.

Secondary sources which itself are dependent on primary sources are also discussed. For quotations, citations and to derive interpretation we have referred to secondary sources. By cross checking both the primary and secondary sources we have analysed our topic to a great extent. To understand the rites and rituals, festivals in Meitei Hindu (Hindu Manipuri) society we have to rely mainly on secondary sources. The continuity and change, the impact of Vaishnavism and the comparative studies can be discussed with the help of secondary sources. For instance, Saroj Nalini Parrot's, "The Religion of Manipur, (Pub. 1980,

Calcutta) puts emphasis on the developments of Manipuri Hinduism, specially in Chaitanya Vaishnavism from Navadwip in Bengal becoming the accepted official religion of the Manipur court and people, as well as certain side-lights into other aspects of Hinduism (e.g., the worship of Shiva and Durga). The book also thoroughly discusses the rites and rituals performed by the Meitei community after converting into Vaishnavism. By the help of proper analysis of the prevailing chronicles published empathised Cheitharol Kumbaba and Ningthourol Lambuba, we can initiate cross cultural studies between the Meities and the Kuki, Naga and the Bishnupriyas. The following published books are also focus on our works.

### Secondary Source

1. Khunung Lichat; Sajat T. Madhop Singh and N. Khelchandra Singh, 1969.
2. Religion of Manipur; Shakespeare, 1913.
3. Festivals of India; Bijendra Nath Sharma.
4. Bijaya; Lakshmi Brara.
5. History of Manipur; Gangmumei Kabui, 1991.

### Table 1.1: Cultural Aspects

| *Sl. No.* | *Salai* | *Ancestor Worship* | *Days/Months for Worship* | *Leaves Used As Dishes* | *Colours Represen-ting the Clans* | *Name of the Clan Lady* | *Water Taken for Offering* | *Types of Daos* |
|---|---|---|---|---|---|---|---|---|
| | (A) | (B) | (C) | (D) | (E) | (F) | (G) | (H) |
| 1. | Ningthouja | Pakhangba | 15th day of Inga (June-July) | Thamna-Khenjong (Lotus Leaf) | Red | Wangamlon | Nungjeng Pukhri | Chakthang |
| 2. | Luwang | Piyainu | 12th day of Wakching (December-January) | Layai (Banana Leaf) | Blue | Yoirumion | Lamphel Lake | Tondumba |
| 3. | Angom | Khakpa Ningthou Chanu | 12th day of Ingen (July-August) | Layai (Banana Leaf) | White | Nongbaion | Kongba Mairombi | Pukthang |
| 4. | Khuman | Piyainu | Tuesday on the full moon day of Sajibu (April) | Kwakla (Leaf of a particular species of banana) | Black | Khuyoirol | Pumlen Lake | Tonkakpa |
| 5. | Chenglei | Huimu Leima | 26th day of Phairen (February) | Thamma (Lotus Leaf) | Grey | Kambong Ningol | Takyel | Khuthokthang |

(*Contd.*)

(Contd.)

| Sl. No. | Salai | Ancestor Worship | Days/Months For Worship | Leaves Used As Dishes | Colours Represen-ting The Clans | Name of the Clan Lady | Water Taken for Offering | Types of Daos |
|---|---|---|---|---|---|---|---|---|
| | (A) | (B) | (C) | (D) | (E) | (F) | (G) | (H) |
| 6. | Khaba-Nganba | Puroi Lemnusuk (Nganba) | Sunday morning of the 19th day of Kalen (May-June) | Laihoula (A leaf similar to turmeric leaf) | Violet | Khabarol | Loitang | Chinaiba |
| 7. | Moirang | Ngangsabi | 12th day of Lamda (March) | Khangra (Leaf of a particular tree called Khangra) | Yellow | Iwanglon | Loktak Lake | Yenbatok |

# 2
# Naming of the Months

Every region and religion has a custom-made calendar that reflects the diversity of culture and tradition it represents. Most are designed to accommodate specific festivals and religious rituals; they are also symbols of generations of different intellectual, philosophical and cultural evolution. At the same time every community in the world has a lore to explain how its months were named. Thus there is the lore that January was named after the Roman God Janus, the two-faced God of doors; February was named after Februa, the feast of expiation, etc. In the case of the Manipuris, there is a book which tries to explain how the twelve months of the calendar were named. This book is called Tharon.[1]

---

1. R.K. Jhalajit Singh, *A History of Indian Literature*, Vol. I (From the 18th century to 1700 AD). pp. 98-101.

Tharon literally means the lore of the months. 'Tha' is known as the months and 'Lon' is the lore. Moreover, 'Tha' is also traditionally known as the moon.[2] The twelve months of the Manipuri calendar with their corresponding Bengali and English months are given below:

| *Manipuri Calendar* | *Bengali Months* | *English Months* |
|---|---|---|
| Sajibu | Chaitra-Baishakh | March-April |
| Kalen | Baishakh-Jaishtha | April-May |
| Inga | Jaishtha-Asar | May-June |
| Ingen | Asar-Shravan | June-July |
| Thawan | Shravan-Bhadra | July-August |
| Langban | Bhadra-Ashwin | August-September |
| Mera | Ashwin-Kartik | September-October |
| Hiyanggei | Kartik-Agrahayan | October-November |
| Poinu | Agrahayan-Pausa | November-December |
| Wakching | Pausa-Magha | December-January |
| Phairen | Magha-Phalgun | January-February |
| Lamda | Phalgun-Chaitra | February-March |

As also mentioned above, in Tharon, the counting of the months begins from Lamda, roughly March. The book calls it the first month. This shows that originally the Manipuri year began in spring in Lamda. Now, in the present Manipuri calendar, it is the twelfth month. Explaining how Sajibu was named, Tharon says "The immortal source of all gods and maker of the earth grows

2. M.S. Tharon.

horns in this month very well; so this month is called Sachiphoi". Many prominent scholars interpret 'Tharon' in different way. Some of them are discussed below:

Atombapu Vidyaratna gave an astronomical interpretation to this legend. The bull referred to in this legend is the sun. The carcass of the bull is the warmthless, dim orb of the sun. As winter sets in, dense fog begins to appear in the morning. The sun seems to be unable to dispel it. Evenings, too, become progressively colder. Even if the sun is in the sky at noon, there is no longer sufficient warmth in the sunshine so the sun appears to be dead. It is the carcass of the bull mentioned in the legend. After the autumnal equinox, the warmthless sun drifts day after day in the sky towards the southern horizon. This is the meaning of the carcass of the bull drifting down the Imphal River which on account of the topography of the Manipur valley, flows from the north to the south. But is the sun really dead? Oh, no! we must not despair. After the winter solstice, it seems to stir a little coming towards the north again. So, in the legend the carcass wags its tail. As more time passes after the winter solstice, the life in the sun is noticeable much more easily — the carcass wags its tail all the more.

The month in which the incident narrated in the legend 'happened' is called Poinu. The winter solstice falls in this month. It is interesting to note that the essence of this legend occurs in old Bengali literatures, also. This legend, when it occurs in old Bengali literature, takes the following form:

The supreme Being (Dharma) desired to test as to which of his three sons, Brahma, Vishnu and Shiva, knows his might. So he assumed the semblance of a decomposed carcass and drifted down the river, Balluka. Brahma could not recognise him and allowed the carcass to float down. Vishnu, too, could not recognise him and did the same thing. But Shiva recognised his father and pulled the carcass up. The Supreme Being was very much pleased with his youngest son.[3] Subsequently further research might show that Bengali literature and Manipuri literature got this legend from a common source.

According to John Parrot[4] the months are interpreted as follows:

---

3. Atombapu Sharma *'Manipur Itihas'* Vol. I, Pub. 1942, p. 18.
4. Notes on Meitei (Manipuri) belief and customs, Compiled and Edited by Dr. John Parrot. Pub. Manipur State Archive, Directorate of Art and Culture, Govt. of Manipur, India, pp. 103, 148-149.

| *Month-Names* | | |
|---|---|---|
| 1. | Sajibu or Sajipu | sa(ma) chi-pu(thaba) "mud as deep as a bullock's horn |
| 2. | Kalen | Ka(ba)-len(ba) "heated-pass" |
| 3. | Inga | I-ngan(iba)-"water-stay" |
| 4. | Ingen | I-nga(iba) "water-excessive" |
| 5. | Thawan | tha(ba)-wan(ba) –"planting-waiting or end" |
| 6. | Langban | lang(ba)-pan(ba)-"trouble-stop" i.e. cultivation labour over. Also called CHINGJIN LANGBAN, i.e. like coming to the end of a hill (ching) |
| 7. | Mera | mei-ra(kpa) – "rice-some" cf.meiruk |
| 8. | Hiyanggei | hiyang-kei-"boat race-granary" |
| 9. | Poinu | phou-(a)nou(ba)-"rice-new" |
| 10. | Wakching | (a)wa(ngba)-ching-"high-hill" referring to the heaps of rice in the granaries |
| 11. | Phairen | phai(ba)-ren(ba)-"stop-pass": the storing of rice is over and the new rice can be taken out of the granaries. Also known as LANA PHAIREN (langa, try: i.e. try your best to collect grain again, by beginning to cultivate) |
| 12. | Lamda | Lam-ta(ba)-"field-fall", i.e. when the ploughs and bullocks come into the fields again |

Pandit Achouba,[5] a prominent local scholar, put emphasis on the religious themes underlying the months in the following way:

| | |
|---|---|
| Sajibu | Also called CHENBI-from sa (animal), or cow, ji, horn, bhu, break (phobia). The creator broke the horn of a cow, which supported the world at this time. |
| Kalen | Also called KAMBI. All gods prevented (khamba) the creator from coming down to earth at this time. |
| Inga | Also called the ASAUTHA (tha, month). From i, blood, ngangba, red. The six khonjomnubis went to heaven, giving blood red leisnam, to show the time. From the sight of the husbands of the six Loinai saphabas this period was called Inga. |
| Ingen | Also called HARENG THA. The time when evil deities were placated with blood. |
| Thawan | From thou, work, wanba, to do. At the time of the creation the goddess, Leimaren, did her work with difficulty. |
| Langbal | Also called ACHIT. From langba, to give offerings, outside. The time when flowers and fruits were offered to the creator by all men. |

5. Ibid, p. 148.

**Mera** Also called AREM THA. From machi, horn, ratpa, to worship. The destroyer of creation was worshipped with horns in this month.

**Hiyanggei** Also called CHIKTHAM. From hi, jewel, yang(yai), gem, kei, storehouse. The god Koubaren returned the valuables and secret things which remained after the creation.

**Poinu** Also called UNTHAM. From poi, traveler, nu, woman. Atiya Guru Sidaba came, disguised as Phouoibi, to his three sons, to see who would recognise him. Only the youngest son discerned that the poirakpa nupi was not a woman but their father. Atiya Guru Sidaba trusted and kept his youngest son.

**Wakching** Also called AWAO THA. From wak (wa), trouble, ching, mountain. The Guru at the time of creation was united to Leimaren and named her Warabi Chinglen.

**Phairen** Also called ASIT THA. From phaire, lived, because the Guru lived to give the souls of all creation.

**Lamta** Also called THABI or KUMBI. From lam, earth, taba, fall, because in the time of creation all seeds fell on earth. THABI is from thaba, sow, piba, give, because at this time the Goddess Leimaren sowed seeds for all creation. KUMBI is from kum, year, piba give meaning the first month of the year.

Upendra Nath Chakravarti[6] stated that the year is divided into months according to the progress of agricultural operations, from which the months take their names as follows:

| | |
|---|---|
| Lamda | derived from lam, land, taba, to fall, i.e. the month in which ploughing begins (Yumjao concurs). |
| Sajibu | derived from san, cattle, machi, horn, puthaba go down i.e. the month in which the cattle's horns are covered with dust, showing that progress has been made with ploughing. (Yumjao gives puthaba the more usual meaning of "to be boggy", and says the name means the month when the mud is as deep as a cow's horn). |
| Kalen | derived from kaba, to bake, lenba to pass the time i.e. the month when the heat of the sun dries the fields (Yumjao concurs). |
| Inga | derived from ising, water, nganba, to be plentiful i.e. the north when the rains break (Yumjao concurs). |

6. Ibid, p. 149.

| | |
|---|---|
| Thawan | derived from thaba, to plant, wanba, to be short of (or to end), i.e., the worker of transplanting is nearing its end (Yumjao concurs). |
| Langban | derived from langba, to be busy or troubled, panba, to stop, i.e. when the first stage of the trouble of cultivation is over. This month is also called CHINGJIN LANGBAN. Chingjin is derived from ching, hill, machin, face or front. This refers to the surmounting of difficulties (Yumjao says, as when coming over a hill, the trouble of the climb has been surmounted). |
| Mera | derived from mei, rice, lakpa, to come i.e. the harvesting of the early autumn rice begins in this month (Yumjao concurs-for mei, rice, cf., meiruk). |
| Hiyanggei | derived from Hiyang, boat race, kei, granary, i.e. the month in which the boat race was held and men progressed with their harvest (Yumjao concurs). |
| Poinu | derived from phou, paddy, anouba, new, i.e. the month of the new paddy. It is also called Poinu Langban indicating the end of the second troublesome stage of cultivation, the harvest. (Yumjao concurs). |
| Wakching | derived from wangba, high, ching, hill, i.e. the month when the paddy is stored in the granaries in heaps tapering to a point like the hills (Yumjao concurs). |

Phairen derived from phaiba, lenba, to pass the time, i.e. the prohibition against taking paddy out of the granary has passed. This month is also called LANGA PHAIREN, meaning that when Phairen has passed the cultivator should be ready to plough his fields again (The meaning to this month is not very clear: Yumjao says that langa means "to try").

### Meitei Calendar

| *Sl. No.* | *Rites & Rituals/Festivals* | *Months* |
|---|---|---|
| 1. | Saroi Khangba | Lamda (Feb.-March) |
| 2. | Yaosang (Holi) | -do- |
| 3. | Laikeithel Kaba | -do- |
| 4. | Ancestor worship of Moirang | 2nd day of Lamda (Feb.-March) |
| 5. | Kongba Leithong Phatpa | 7th day of Lamda (Feb.-March) |
| 6. | Cheiraoba | Sajibu (March-April) |
| 7. | Ancestor worship of Khuman | Full moon day of Sajibu (March-April) |
| 8. | Ancestor worship of Khaba Nganba | 10th day of Kalen (April-May) |
| 9. | Ancestor worship of Ningthouja | 15th day of Inga (May-June) |
| 10. | Koorak Lamtaiba | Inga (May-June) |
| 11. | Kang Chingba (Rath Jatra) | 2nd July of Ingen (June-July) |
| 12. | Krishna Astami | Ingen (June-July) |
| 13. | Ancestor worship of Angom | 12th day of Ingen (June-July) |
| 14. | Tarpan | Langban (Aug.-Sept.) |
| 15. | Heiku Hitongba | 14th day of Langban (Aug.-Sept.) |

| | | |
|---|---|---|
| 16. | Kwak Tanba | 14th day of Langban (Aug.-Sept.) |
| 17. | Mera Mentongba | Mera (Sept.-Oct.) |
| 18. | Mera Haochongba | -do- |
| 19. | Mera Shantuba | -do- |
| 20. | Mera Wa yungba | -do- |
| 21. | Mera Wa phukpa | -do- |
| 22. | Hi Tanaba (boat racing ceremony) | Hiyangei (Oct.-Nov.) |
| 23. | Phaobi Khurumba | Poinu (Nov.-Dec.) |
| 24. | Ancestor worship of Luwang | 12th day of wakching (Dec.-Jan.) |
| 25. | Loutaba | Phairen (Jan.-Feb.) |
| 26. | Ancestor worship of Chenglei | 26th day of Phairen |

# 3
# Sharoi Khangba

Of the series of rites and rituals performed in a Meitei calendar year, Sharoi-khangba is the first ritual held in the first month of the year. In Tharon, an incident in Meitei text dealing with the origin and evolution of the ancient Meitei Calendar year, Lamda is enshrined as Thapi cheihoutha, meaning the first or initial month of the year. Following the ancient tradition, the Sharoi Khangba ritual is still performed in the month of Lamda even though this erstwhile first month has now slided to the twelfth month of the year.

There has been an age-old belief among the Meiteis that on the night of the first Saturday of the month of Lamda, all the Umanglais, the gods of the countryside, assemble together and prepare a list of persons who are going to die and those who are going to survive the ensuing year. Those who are included in the list of the dead are counted by their respective names each of them represented by a piece of stick. This process of counting of persons who could die with pieces of stick is known as Shingtek-Shingthaba. As it is believed that those who are included in the Shingtek-Shingthaba would die within that year, these deities are worshipped with offerings by the people to escape from the list of the dead. Such an appeasement rite is known as Sharoi-Khangba. The word Sharoi means the attendants of both presiding deities of all directions and other divinities and the word "Khangba" denotes offerings of food to these attendants. The Sharois are polydaermonists and are also known by the name of Loyuin-Khamyin. In the ritual, not only the Sharois but also the principal gods and goddesses, the ten presiding deities of all directions are worshipped with due incantations and offerings invoking their blessings for the prosperity and welfare of the community for the coming year. The primary objective of this ritual is to please the sarois to drive away the evils. There are two types of saroi khangba. One is state saroi Khangba and another one is local Saroi Khangba. The former is held in the palace by the order of the kings. Inside the palace there are temples and places of the deities known as the lamingthous Nongsaba, the Ibudhou Pakhangba, the goddess Yumjao lairemma and made god 'lainingthou sanahamahi', the male and female deities known as 'Yangdouba' and 'Yangdoubi' at tanyeishang (The office where the officers on duty measure time with water clock). The officers on duty in the royal offices change the dresses and costumes of these deities and worship them with offerings.

The local 'Sharoui Khangba' is the one which is performed in the locality, in the peripherals or in the countryside by the people themselves. In the countryside Sharoi-Khangba is usually performed by elderly women at the outskirts of the villages where two or more roads meet. In this ritual, various articles of food, such as, seven varieties of fruits, similarly a number of flowers, rice, flour, salads prepared from meddler plant with fermented fish, cotton swabs, tobacco leaves, rice, salt chilly etc. are offered to the Sharois. Over and above the articles noted above, certain other articles like a Sareng Fish, an earthen pitcher, ladle, tongs, a three legged iron device and the leaves of Khoiju Leikham plants in an earthen vessel are included in the case of state observance of Sharoi-Khangba performed by the royal maiba (pandits) at the outskirts of the four villages viz. Khurai, Wangkhei, Khwai and Yaiskul. The respective sides of the ritual are at Khurai Lamdaipung (the present Telepati area), Wangkhei Lamdaipung (Lourembam pungthak), at

Khwai Lamdaipung (Wangthombi Lamdaipung) and Yaiskul Lamdaipung (Kakwa Lamdaipung). The deities worshipped in these rituals are Marjing, Wangbren, Koubru and Thangjing respectively. After completing the rituals, the maibas then return to the maiba sanglen (Institution) at the royal enclosure and report the matter to the three principal maibas who greet them singing a hymn known as khoju Lam-Ok[1], while offerings are made to the deities in the ritual of Sharoi-Khangba, the following hymn is chanted:

> *Hey laibungthou mapan lainura taret, umanglai, sharoi humphumathoimak, nakhoigi nachinjak heiram taret, leiram taret, kabok nachan taret, pukyu waiyu, heibi mana singju, cheng chak, taibang panbagi chari thakliba pumnamak perabane, masi chaduna kum ashigi phatta houdi pumnamak ngakpiyu shembiyu.*

O Nine laibungthous, O seven lainuras umanglais and sixty-one Sharois. We offer you all edible things, please take our offerings and shower happiness and prosperity upon us, removing all the evils and calamities that might befall us this year. After the Sharois are propitiated with offerings of food, all the ten guardian deities (or directional deities) of different directions are worshipped, one after another uttering

1. MS Sana Lamok.

their respective prayers and hymns. They are being worshipped to bestow good harvests and for the prosperity and well being of the people and the country. First of all god Koubru is invoked with the following utterings[2]:

*Hey ipu koubaren-o kouba leimacha kounu leimacha kakyai phamkhiba anglounakamba tekpi chingne tekpi khabuk tanglei ching, manai taba eya panchallam sekwai taddan pung senching chingnungpok chingsa napom taramanga phangbabu khunetnaba loimanai khunda hanba, charik mapan thaba nongthei ma-u lingba, untruk iriba wautaruk ithaba laiyingthou-o naphou nangan pan nahei narong panbabu teina sembirak-o*

*Hey ipu thongnang ningthou, thongnang chingbu tanna khanba, thongnang malei ching lindu yangtek chingi mende ningthou saraba mende nungol ching, ningna keisi ching, laikham sumdompok haonu lagoubi langouba phana ching, mangthom lokhaoreng nareng chingbu tanna*

*Khaba laiyingthou, haomarokki khambi phanba thoudu nongpok leppa naphou nangan panbu teina sembirak-o, nahei narong panbu teina sembirak-o, nahei narong*

2. MS Pongning.

*panbu teina sembirak-o, nahei narong panbu teina sembirak-o nanongyaisingbu kubiyu yengbiyu.*

*Hey ipu hangoi hingthou atiya sidaba-o salammanganba kamba salamba nama tingba nignthou sambu maharaba, nanamna yangbi oi, napukna nongthou oi, taibang nongsapanabu sembiba laiyingthou-o amamba thoudaba anganba wahenba yaba kongkhangsagi namu pongbu thoutamba namupngdi tha tara samok tha tara, sagol tha tara sandang tha tara, hameng tha*

*manga ok tha manga hui tha ahum, nganu tha ama, yen tha ama, khunu tha ama miran pnglam salam manbu teina sekhiba thongjao lairekien achanba khoimom lamithubu kanarambu tana khanba naphou nangan jpan nahei narong panbu teina sempirak-o kubi-o yengbi-o.*

*Hey ipu thanthong ningthou-o, chaobasu koiren ningthou-o koiren ahum thongatpada watamba, petpi petthangne, singjangwa khaine, wakhai ningthou manganba pammaru chingoi oinam ching leimayai-thambal nongsarou kege singjamphai, thanga tonba ningthou u-thabal namnganba loktak khongaonaba, nungmu tumba mangdabada khunetnaba nungbi sidababu khudanaba thangjing kon maru yaioiba lainingthou-o*

*Naphou-nangan pan, nahei narong panbu teina sembirok-o, lairen nanongyai nasu hebongthou hebemnasingbu kubi-o yengbi-o, he ipu mahouningthou wangbren khana chaoba phamdanlongbu tallakhanba manbi nungtekmana khikamyokna.*

*Khikpadi sanyai lanyai khikkatle thumna-o chamasu loigi loimalle, yennao chamasu hupna noigi noimalle pangi pangsingkhiye, nahanubi nungda pakna taina chakyen.*

*Hourabagi enba nanu lukthak-nungda hanu luktheektrabagi lingam laikam laibu laikhungle, hanu luktheklabada linkamlaibu laikokle, laikok chingda wanganba laiyingthyou naphou nangan pan nahei narong panbu teina sethirak-o he khuman muyek pakhangba kubi-o.*

*Hey ipu util ningthou-ukang ningthou-o khoubuwakan khourenna tille, tubu nangi laihui chingbu tanna khanba malang khongaonaba tillang khoisitnaba nongpok malang humoibabu samu tungoiba sanglou ningna tenaba*

*Laiyingthou-o naphou nangan jpan nahei narong panbu teina seitharak-o nanong yaisingna punemjariye.*

*Hey ipu nongkhongba selloi mabu tana khanba selloi nakpakma selloi tukup pureiching teinou yotpihuitha ching, charik mapan thaba nongthei ma-u lingba chingbu tanna khanba kabo senbi ngaiyonaba naphou nangan pan nahei narong panbu teina sembirak-o.*

*Hey ipu thangwai nongpok yairung atambada chingu natte heiba, saren tangam yada chikpa kangjei humdang nareng suba nongpok mallang hummoiba langoi moisa ya ayangbabu nasu hebungthou hebbemmasing punemjari.*

*Hey sidaba mapu leinung thongaren ahanba-o asiba chamma nongdamba achangba chamma nongkhaiba thoutha sinthong heiba achungba chamma thong hangba ashiba lhamma thongthingba amansingkum lallam sinba nang asi thong thingbi-o achangbagibu thong hangbi-o.*

*Hey kasa nongthou soraren khakpa nignthou panjumba kasa paotak heiba awang thangwai yoirengba korou thakta thoudaba wangban thakta watemba nangbu punemuariye.*

*Hey maigei ngakpa laningthou tarama nakhoina nongaiyaida makhoi tongbabu pinabiram-o.*

The incantation is written in archaic Manipur language praising the ten directional deities or sovereign Gods also known as Ningthou Pongba Tara (Tei Kings) who guard different directions of Manipur. We have translated only the first three paras because the remaining are the same (See Appendix 1).

# 4
# Yaosang (Holi)

Among the festivals of the Meiteis yaosang is the greatest. It is a five-day festival beginning from the full-moon day of Lamda (Feb.-March) and Phalgun in Bengali month. Though, originally a religious festival of the Hindus, the gaiety produced by this spring festival is so infectious that people belonging to other religions take part in it as well. Whatever may be the origin of the Hindu festival there is no gainsaying the fact that it is in essence and spirit a spring festival. It celebrates the advent of spring. The influence of this pleasant season is evident on both animate and inanimate objects. People enjoy with gay abundance the vital feelings of delight created by the revival of nature all around. To a community with a predominantly agricultural economy, the successful completion of agricultural operations is an event to rejoice over. The festival is held at a time when the harvest is over, the granary is full, the hearts are content and the season is at its best. The myth behind celebrating holi in North India relates to Holika sitting in a fire with the boy Prahlad, a devotee of Vishnu, in her lap with the intention of burning him. Prahlad, due to his devotions is saved while Holika is burnt. But the myth behind Holi in Manipur is completely different from that of the rest of North India This myth is, in fact, borrowed from Bengal from where the particular sect of Hinduism (Gauriya Vaishnavism) came.

The preparation of the festival begins well in advance. The night before the actual festival is marked with making of bonfires, which is known as Nonglaoba. In Nonglaoba the young boys abuse each other with obscene words, a practice fairly widespread in connection with fertility festival. Shakespeare points out that it was traditionally used in connection with the exchanges between the God and Goddess Nongpok Ningthou and Panthoibi. However, modern enlightened opinion is not in favour of this practice, which is being gradually given up with the spread of education.

The celebration of the festival is set off with the burning of a small hut constructed with bamboos and thatch in their respective villages or leikais (locality) just after the sunset. After the burning of the huts with elaborate ritual, people collect the half-burnt bamboos and fix them at their gates. It is believed that these half-burnt bamboos ward off evil spirits. They also put the ash from the burnt flags on their foreheads. The Vaishnava elders generally abstain from cooked food till the Yaosang (hut) is lighted. Although fish is a favourite food to the Manipuri Hindus, it is the practice to give vegetarian food even to small children on this day. Soon after the hut is burnt the young boys and girls, even the aged men and women, go on begging for gifts in cash and kind like rice and vegetable from door to door and from passerbys for their feast. The main programme of the festival, which is generally associated, is Thabal Chongba, an ancient folk dance. The expression literally means jumping in the moonlight. Both sexes, irrespective of age take part and the participants join hands in a circle, songs which describe the creation, famous legendary exploits and love stories are sung to the accompaniment of music in chorus led by a leader or an elder as it often happens when youth and pleasure meet. Thabal chongba is a regular feature of the Holi festival. The dancing continues until late night. Thabal Chongba is a regular feature of the Holi festival.

The ancient manuscript reveals out that this folk dance is performed in the form of Lairen Mathek Chingba (Python's course).[1] It is a depiction of the coiling design of Pakhangba, the mythical King of Manipur. This particular dance is traditionally known as Augri Hanggen chongba, which is a part of the creation of myth. The tradition of Thabla Chonbgba is the festival of Yaosang is still in vogue.

1. Lousie Lightfoot, *Dance-Rituals of Manipur*, India, pp. 38-40.

# 5
# Lai Keithel Kaba

Lai Keithel Kaba is a festival celebrated at the temple of Shree Shree Bijoygovinda. It is being held annually on the twentieth Lamda (Feb.-March). On this occasion, group of people from different places come to the royal palace and gather together and then the congregation led by the king, on horse and elephants, proceeds to the temple of Shree Shree Bijoygovinda situated at Sagolband (Imphal west districts). Before the arrival of the king at the temple, the image of Govindaji is brought out and kept at the open space in front of the temple where all the rituals are being carried out. In the latter part of the eighteenth century, the then king Anantasai was in-charge of the Shree Shree Bijoygovindaji temple. It was during his reign, that the Holi and Halangkar festivals of Baishnavism were introduced and celebrated simultaneously with Lai Keithel Kaba at the temple ground of Shree Shree Bijoygovinda. This festival centred on the cult of Pakhangba, an indigenous deity, in which an effigy made of straw is burnt in the same way as the effigy of the monstress Holika is burnt. The burning of effigy is known as Charoimei Thaba and also suggests a compromise between the two religions, one which is foreign and another indigenous. Like the Egyptians, the Iranians and the Chinese who reckon their calendar from the spring season, the Meiteis are also stated to have begun the reckoning of the calendar from the month of Lamda (Feb.-March) which corresponds, according to Rashtria Panchang published by the Government of India, with the Baishak, the first month of Hindu calendar.

Another interesting aspect of the festival of Lai Keithel Kaba is the ritual carried out by the nobles of the four leikais (village circles) at a particular place called Lamjao Ngamdai which is said to be a place where deities namely Tangja Lila Khwai Tubi Lainingthou and Kanglel. Muhi Pakhangba frequently haunt, in honour of Lai Nura Taret, a group of seven female deities and Laibungthou Mapan, a group of nine male deities. This is also said to be a place of Khwai Nungjeng Piba, a mythical hero of the story-Numit Kappa. The most important part of the festival is the representation of the eight female deities namely[2]: i. Pukshinkhombi, ii. Angaibi, iii. Thongaibi, iv. Thingbailoikhombi, v. Thareima, vi. Kotingleima, vii. Chengleima and viii. Yuchengleima as if they were selling things at a market place, and the offerings of Sana Lupa Kanyai Hunba, (small pieces of gold and silver and also parched rice). The parched rice offered in the rituals differs from one Salai (clan) to another. The following are the different rices of the seven salais or clans:

| *Clan* | *Name of the Rice* |
|---|---|
| Angom | Phouren, Noining |
| Ningthouja | Phouren, Phoujao |
| Luwang | Yenthic, Sangsangba |
| Khuman | Tumai, Chahao Poireiton |
| Moirang | Moirangphou, Taothabi |
| Khaba Nganba | Phougak Sajikkhong, Changlei |
| Chenglei | Sangsangba, Phouren Noining |

Further in the festival the foodstuff sold by eight female deities are brought and cooked; and then, it was arranged into eight Chakluks (shares). The prepared eight Chakluks represent eight Pibas (males): Mangang, Luwang, Khuman, Angom, Moirang, Khaba

2. Naorem Sanajaoba, *Manipur Past and Present*, Vol. II, Article by Koijam Diren: Festivals of Manipur. p. 246.

Nganba and Wangbi. The addition and grouping of these Chakluks in sequence is known as Salai Luptinba.

While observing the rite of Salai Luptinba, people sing the hymn of Mihourol. Then, the king's courtiers, four Leikai Lakpas, four Pana Lakpas, all Salai Pibas and the whole people make a promise in order to rule the country in peace and harmony. This rite is a sort of festival that aims at bringing a peaceful co-existence between the gods-community and human group as well as among individuals. The festival, really, manifests as to how to exist in cooperation by forgetting the pride, variety and selfishness among each other. It also introduced the feature of keithel kaba (marketing) by human beings. The main objective of the ritual is to make people live peacefully throughout their life. The ritual of Lai Keithel Kaba, though based on a certain myth, had deep political significance.

# 6
# Ancestor Worship of Moirang Clan

The ancestor worship, the Burmese Buddhism and the Hindu cults have been welded together in the Meitei religion whose aim is the realisation of God and His reflection in human beings. Before we proceed to the rituals of ancestor worship of different clans the detailed explanation about the clans in Meitei society is very necessary. In Manipur, since the ancient periods, there were a number of principalities led by Chiefs (see Map). Each had different settlement pattern. They had their distinct cultural affinity during the various periods. In course of time these different cultural affinities were merged into Meitei society. Their cultural affinity is still preserved in the rites and rituals of Apokpa Khurumba (ancestor worship).[1] From this ritual we can know that the water for offering to the Gods and ancestors was taken and brought from different lakes, e.g. Moirang took water as an "offering" item from the Loktak lake, Khuman took from Pumlen pat (lake),[2] Ningthouja from Nungjeng, Luwang from Lamphel Pat, Angom from Kongba Mairombi, Chenglei from Takyelpat, KhabaNganba from Loitang Pat (Pat is traditionally known as Loktak).

These customs still prevail in their ancestor worship or Apokpa Khurumba. These lakes represent seven clans and show the different principalities in possession of settlement of different clans. The people surrounding the lakes generated income from the said lakes. That is why these lakes were so much important in their livelihood. Not only water they also used different flowers and fruits, even the firewood, which are closely related to their ancestor – worship, especially of the seven clans (See Table). In addition to this, they had different colours of clanial cloth and different typical Thang (Thang is the traditional name of dow).

---

1. N. Khelchandra, *Khunung Lichat Sazat*, Pub. 1967, p. 7.
2. Ibid, p. 20.

### 2. Khuman

Khuman principality was established in the south of Imphal covering the eastern portion of the Loktak lake, Pumlen Pat and their adjoining areas including Thoubal and Mayang Imphal.[3] At first their capital was at Thoubal. Later it was shifted to Mayang Imphal.[4] Some of the important chiefs were: i) Poreiton, ii) Sidapung, iii) Arong, iv) Tumaba, v) Lungba, vi) Lungba Ahanba, etc.

### 3. Moirang

The Moirang principality established in south western part of Manipur covered Loktak lake and the present day places like Kumbi, Ngangkha, Kwakkta, Thanga and their adjoining areas. To the south it extended upto Phaugakchao. Moirang was also known as Kege. Kege and Ngagoi, both villages, were known as parts of Moirang. In fact, the territory was identified as Kege-Moirang, the place where the two communities, already known by their names, lived together and also administered their domain together. Some chiefs of

---

3. N. Khelchandra Singh Sabhapati Basant, *MSP Imphal* 1983, p. 7.
4. Khelchandra Singh, *Chada Laihui*, 1966, p. 19.

Moirang are i) Hamsa ii) Phang Phang iii) Sunucha iv) Ahong Khamsa v) Mayang Loikinpa vi) Sana Rakhwa etc.

### 4. Ningthouja/Mangangs

Ningthouja identified with Mangangs settled in Imphal valley. Their area comprised of a territory about three miles in radius. Important rivers associated with their territory are the Nambul and Naga rivers and few small tributaries like Kongba, Makuging and Yaishen, etc. Kangla was their capital. It covered roughly one square mile.[5] The Chiefs were i) Nongda Lairen Pakhangba ii) Khyoi Tompok iii) Taothingmang iv) Khui Ningomba v) Pangsiba vi) Kaokhangba, etc.

### 5. Chenglei

The Chenglei principality was established to the south western side between Moirang and Ningthouja boundary. Its boundary covered the modern Takyelpat, Tabungkhok, Heinou Khongnembi, etc. Important rivers associated with them are Nambul Merakhong,[6] etc. Some of the chiefs of Chenglei were i) Tharong ii)

5. N. Khelchandra Singh, *Chada Laihui*, 1966, p. 19.

6. Ibid, p. 3.

Yuchiklai iii) Yukangkon iv) Saraton v) Sarapuktang vi) Saramei vii) Thangyce Khongchromba, etc.

### 6. Angom

Angoms settled at Nongmaiching hill. Their capital was at Puleiromba Khongnangkhong. Their coronation used to take place where, at present C.C. Higher Secondary School campus is situated.[7] Iril and Kongba river passed through their territory. Their sacred place was Kongba Meirombi from where they still use water for their ancestor worship. Some important chiefs of Angoms were i) Pureiromba ii) Khamnung iii) Iwaithang iv) Chingmit Yoirenba v) Ahong Khamsa vi) Tontou, etc.

### 7. Khaba Nganba

The Khaba-Nganba ethnic community ruled from the Kangla area. Their principality comprised of territories around Kangla. This zone was central to all other principalities. For their rituals they collected water from the Nungjeng Pukhri inside the Kangla. When they had been defeated by Pakhangba and were forced to move out of their capital they migrated to the hills

7. Ibid, p. 11.

and merged themselves with the hill people. Though scattered in different directions these people retained their ethnic identity. We learnt that later they controlled the Loitang lake and its adjacent areas. The rivalry between them and Pakhangba had led to the disintegration of the Khaba Nganba clan.

For Moirang they worship their ancestor on the 12th day of Kalen (May-June). Their deity is Ngansabi (see Table 1). The offering items are water from Loktak lake, Leishang Flower (Seligendelia species), khangra (a kind of plant leaf as dish), fire from two-fold of flames. Leikhamwai Napu Nashen (a small plant) is used for sprinkling water, yenbatok dao (Dao made in the shape of hen head) is used as their Clan sword; red strip Sareng (a typical fish) use as their offering fish: Heiba fruit (ficus species) and Ching Enseen (a hilly plant) is used as firewood.[8]

In the Apokpa Khuramba (ancestor worship), of all the seven clans of the Meitei society, the incantations of Apoklon is compulsory While other hymns such as Anani Athou Laison, Naheiron, Yumdei Naksen and Meigi Tengtha can be used in any

8. N. Khelchandra Singh, *Thainagi Seireng*, 1966, p. 7.

ceremony ritual.[9] The presentation of the Apoklon hymns is given in the following way:

Ha ye tampaka poklibi, tampak thibi tingthou huplahara kongdeng, chana, yemmi, tonglong leashing yangla thoubong satou yengdou charrot phaibang tengna nugmaibiga poklibi nangbu taige haina taina nemsige..........

The above ritual indicates the praising of ancestors or creators of living beings in the universe (See Appendix 2). By worshipping these ancestors, people hope to earn the virtues of sovereign god for their generations. According to legend, performing Apoklon ritual in the ancestor worship gives prosperity, health, wealth and peace of mind to the respective members of the clans. The main objective of this ritual is to appease the Almighty God Creator to live peacefully together without inflicting evil on each other and to give mutual cooperation and remain pro-ecology and environment.

9. Atombapu Sharma, *Manipur Itihas*, Vol. I, 1942, p. 18.

# 7
# Kongba Leithong Phatpa

On the seventh day of Lamda (Feb.-March), the Meitei community performs a rite and ritual called Kongba Leithong Phatpa (digging the hole at kongba). It is a ceremony of prognostication and is ritually ceremonised as Kongba Leithong Phatpa during the reign of Leinung Lonja Ariba. Periodically, there prevails two extraordinary months during a year, which is known as Malamas by the Hindus. Later, in order to commemorate this rite, they place a mark in by shifting it at Kongba. Since then the ceremony had been recognised as Kongba Leithong Phatpa, till date. According to an ancient Meitei text, "Masil", one Guru (preceptor) bore a hole on the surface of the earth and kept all the evils of twelve months in between the nine layers of the earth. Hence, it is known as Leithong Phatpa. Since then this ritual i.e. Leithong Phatpa has been observed as an annual ceremony amongst the Meitie communities.

The actual place of the ritual takes place in a rice field which is located about four kilometres to the east from Imphal between the Iril and Kongba River (See Fig. No. 4a). At that particular place there are two mounds, one lying in the east and the other in the west. They are known as Angom Pokpa and Ningthem Pokpa, respectively.

Having offered the rites and rituals to the deities, the two mounds are dug out until the stone is touched. While digging the mounds if any object comes across, either living or non-living, it is collected by the Maiba (priest). If a snake is found, digging will be stopped without coming in contact with the stone. According to the findings, the Maiba will foretell the omens and fortune of the year. Maiba also will perform an offering in a place situated in southeast direction of the two mounds. The offering is called Khayuom Lakpa and it is made to the deity Nongpok Nignthou. If leech, earthworm and dead snail are found, it is presumed that epidemic of diseases, calamities and misfortune will be experienced during the ensuing year. In case frog, live snail, paddy etc. are found it is considered that the year will be a prosperous one.[10]

10. N. Khelchandra, *Khunung Lichat Sazat*, 1967, p. 9.

The items of offering Kongba Leithong Phatpa are as follows: Two phamphi (cloth stitched at the centre), two Thakan (canopy), four yot khunet (iron peddler), eight coins peddler, two handful of Langthrei (a medicinal plant's leaves), two fruits (having special smell), two Leishang (orchid), ten hand of bananas, ten betel nuts with leaves of pan, some important fruits and sugarcane, Khoiju Leikham (medicinal plant), eight Uchiwa (a small typical bamboo), two earthen plates, two small baskets with full of paddy, cowry, dry-fish, four pair pieces of gold and silver, one salt cake, twenty wax candles, two earthen pots, two sareng (fish), two Ngaten (a typical fish), twenty Ngamu (fish), twenty Nganoi (fish species), twenty kg. of rice, edible oil, five containers of dal, four salt cakes, four utong (container) chilly, ginger, two bunches of firewood, five packs of banana leaves, two thangjou (typical dao), two spades and a coin for the deity.

One winnowing fan for Meiba (local extracting fire), one phamphi (cloth stitch at the centre), one canopy, a full dress of deity, five hand of bananas, one scented fruit, one Leishang (orchid) flower, five wax candle, five Uchiwa (a small typical bamboo), one Sangai (a typical knife), some fruits, sugarcane, a pair of konyaipu (pieces of gold and silver) and earthen jar. Upon these two cloths for wrapping the deity, two

Heiruk (dishes of fresh fruits), two leaves of pan, and five leaves of pan for Meiba are very essential.

Prior to the day of Kongba Leithong Phatpah, the king makes a public avowal in the market that tomorrow would be kongba Leithong phatpa. Therefore, no one would be allowed to dig earth in the four Leikais (localities), i.e. Khwai Yaiskul, Wangkhei, and Khurai. After offering to the deities, the offering items are cooked by the Maiba's party and served as a grand feast.

The Maibas return to the royal palace without making any delay (See Fig. No 4c). However, the villagers are not permitted to, even, passing dung in the area. While returning they accompany two Langthrei leaves which have been already offered to the deities Angom Pokpa and Ningthem Pokpa by wrapping separately by two cloths, encircling around their necks. The two leaves are brought to the enclosures of the palace. In the royal palace the Langthrei leaves are offered at the alter of Yumjao Lairembi (deity) in east and west direction. Then the two leaves are placed and covered by two earthen jars.

After some days it is opened, and, according to the findings, the good and the bad luck of the state is foretold for the ensuing year.

The incantations used by the Maiba (priest) in the rites of Kongba Leithong Phatpa are given below:

(i) Anam Athou

(ii) Naheiron

(iii) Apoklon

(iv) Tudouron

(v) Umanglon

(vi) Iru Laison

(vii) Atai Laison

After spelling out the hymns the Maibas (priests) worship by mentioning the name of the deity.

# 8
# Cheiraoba

Cheiraoba or Sajibu Cheiraoba is a very important ritual of the Meitei. The word is deviated from Sajiphoi. Sajibu is the second month of the Meitei Calendar. The ritual is carried out mainly in honour of Sanamahi, the domestic deity. In the olden days, a man holding a bamboo stick, hanging a bell on the top of it and tied with a flag, went towards each and every street of the place, announcing the end of the forgoing year. 'Chei' literally means stick and Laoba, to announce. So, it has come to be known as 'Cheiraoba' i.e. to announce the end of the year by holding a stick and to welcome the New Year. The Cheiraoba festival, was at first known as Kumg Lakyen Taiba or Sajibu Lakyen Taiba. However, this practice of announcing with stick and bell was discontinued from the time of Kiyambai (1467-1508), the then king of Manipur and a system of Cheithaba was introduced.[1] A man who is assigned the misfortunes of the year on behalf of the king was given the name Cheithaba. The first Cheithaba was Hiyangloi (1484). Cheithaba was exempted from Lallup (State duty) and granted a pari of rice field (2.5 acres) and also an attendant who was also free from Lallup duty. It may also be noted that during his period of one year, the Cheithaba was not supposed to meet the king. In the later period, the practice of granting a pari of land was discontinued and in lieu of it, the king exempted the tax for one pari of Cheithaba's land he owned for his lallup service for his lifetime.

Cheiraoba is observed with a sense of cleanliness. On Cheiraoba every family clean their respective houses. In the morning of Cheiraoba, they offer fresh items of fruits, vegetables, rice, etc. to the household deity Sanamahi and gifts were offered to their elders. The vegetables and rice dust is offered to their household deity, Sanamahi were cooked and offered to the evil spirits outside the gate with enchantments of mantras as given below:

*Lamaba Tumaba Lamsena, Tusenba, Lamgnak-Tungakpa, Lamsen Tusenba, Hanba Kokchao, Hannu*

1. Ibid, p. 49.

*Laikham Laibgung Thou Mapanmak, Lairubataretmak, Umanglai Saroi Humphumathoi Nakhoigi Namingdi Pangan Kou-E Mingkheidi Langpum Kou-E Ashi Korou Numit Ashida Nanaina Katchariba Ashi Chaduna Ngakpio Shenbio Gurugi Yathangne.*

This is a ritual to please the spirits and deities to seek protection from evils. It stars with calling the names of evil spirits-Lamaba tumaba lamsenba, tusenba, lamgnak-temgakpa, lamsenba..... and the nine lords that is Laibungthou Mapan and the sixty one Umanglai Saroi (Forest goddess). Then, request them to eat heartily the food they offer and forgive them from any evil spirit. This is known as Cheiraobagi Lai Chak Thaba (Offering of cooked Food), which is performed with a view to appease the evil spirit. The head of the family, in case he is a male member or any elder living male member of the family or a boy in the absence of an elder man, makes the offerings of the preparations at the family kitchen. The offerings are made at different sites before the members of the family consume the food.

In the Royal Palace such rituals as Saroi Khangba is performed in all four directions in honour of four guardian deities of the Meitei, and the Konok of royal palace reads the results of the planetary position in presence of the king and other royal dignitaries. This is known as Arjmantri Paba (read). The words used by the outgoing cheithaba (See Appendix 3 & 4).

> *Eibu shijaba ibungo laiyingthou nongthouren athoubadi taibang soraren namu pong hanba-o nanai eina puba kum ashibu nanai itaona puba kum ashina leima ningthou punshiba chakhong naohongba lanhong thumhongbabu lepna thoiba henba oirasuno.*

Then they exchange their seats. The outgoing cheithaba sits on the left whereas the incoming on the right side. The person who acts as cheithaba is not permitted to see the king during the year. The king changes a new dress as per option given by the royal scholar and astrologers.

One day before cheiraoba, the Maiba (priest), to Heibokching (Heibok hill) carrying the offerings, which include six inches long reed sticks to adore the deities. This is known as Singtek Singthaba.

For five days people spend their leisure time playing a game of Kang (a traditional indoor game of the Meitei) beginning from the very evening of cheiraoba. This is known as *Silhenba*.

# 9
# Ancestor-Worship of Khuman Clan

Khuman is one of the seven clans of Meitei. They worship their ancestors on Tuesday, the full moon day of sajibu (April). Their maiden deity is Piyainu. The offering items are water from Pumlen Lake, Leishang Flower (Seligendelia species), kwakla (a leaf of a particular species of banana), fire from two-fold of flames. Leikhamwai Napu Nashen (a small plant) is used for sprinkling water, tonkakpa dao is used as their Clan sword; red strip Sareng (a typical fish) used as their offering: Heiba fruit (ficus species) and Ching Enseen (a hilly plant) is used as firewood.[1]

1. Ibid, p. 25.

In this Apokpa Khuramba (ancestor worship), a number of incantations such as Anam Athou Laison, Naheiron, Yumdei naksen laison and Meigi tengtha are used. The following are the hymns of Yumdei naksen laison[2]:

> *Ha mangsok madaimada, phumlen madaimada yatanda, kongdangba taktu madaima senkhong narilma parie hongamagi thanamba nagaira naphamseng nathengan naralli, chasongpham nahongoham mangollom\ng nasunglanhg, nasumang mathennmangi kaomasumarungbu thari lemleimada ha ong ha yeng.*

The above ritual is also one of the essential rituals in ancestor-worship. Yumjao (residential house) for the Meiteis is the abode of the Lais(gods). Hence every stage of house construction is marked by prescribed rituals, auspicious days and dates, and prescribed directions for the whole structure and the rooms. The house structure faces east, and it is believed that if the house faces south or north, some calamity will befall its inhabitants. Hence the above rituals symbolise the proper construction and preservation of house and the cleansing or warding off the evil spirit from the house. The main six parts of the house are mentioned in the

2. Ibid.

rituals. The Maangol (verandah), which is divided into two parts: the right side is called Phamel, where a seat is placed for the head of the family. He receives visitors here. On the left side is mangsok, from where the dead body is taken out. Then the Ningolka, which is the daughter's room and behind that is the room for Leimaren or Yumjao Lairembi, the household goddess. Then comes the room for young children, Thoubunka and finally the kitchen, Chakhumka, which is of course the domain of the women. All these rooms or part of the houses are cleaned on the day of ancestor-worship.

# 10
# Ancestor-Worship of Khaba Nganba Clan

Khaba Nganba is one of the seven clans of Meitei. They worship their ancestor on Sunday, the tenth day of Kalen (April-May). Their maiden deity is Puri-Lamnu-Su. The offering items are water from Laitang Lake, Leishang Flower (Seligendelia species), Leihoura (a kind of plant-leaf for using as dish), fire from two-fold of flames. Leikhamwai Napu Nashen (a small plant) is used for sprinkling water, chinaiba dao (dao horned) is used as their Clan sword; red strip Sareng (a typical fish) used as their offering fish, Heiba fruit (ficus species) and Ching Enseen (a hilly plant) is used as firewood.

In this Apokpa Khuramba (ancestor-worship) are used a number of incantation such as Anam Athou

Laison, Naheiron, Yumdei Naksen and Meigi tengtha. The following are the hymns of the Mei tengtha[1] (see Appendix 5).

> ***chakmom khambi meitrengraba***
> ***meisat meiba met***
> *tektek thoudu met*
> ***kiambi naorei khuna***
> *khoiju tolong mei*
> ***leikham waiba mei***
> *sawang yuphou mei*
> ***poirei khulling mei thangsut meiseng mei***
> ***thoudu nungthang mei***
> *pament allaurlngkon khommang mei*
> *taibang namu pongyokmei*
> *khambi meibun thannamei*
> *lamjao khambi w alnamei melrlk meljao*
> *yaloimei thanga leikal oina mei*
> *chingkhong poireitonna khunthokng*
> *meitei laeima leinao t abina*
> *talbang khulllng mei*
> *ayanglelma lemthong mei*
> *pukcheng kokpa mei*
> *langjeng thumba mei*
> *chakpanubi phuthi mei*

1. MS – Meigi Tengtha Laison.

*hemjengnubi phutha mei*
*chegai kakup mei*
*charu t angsoi mei*
*toumu toljllolj mei*
*singgan nongphal mei*
*lambu tubu mei*
*t aret lalkam mei*
*hemba pamchak mei*
*sadu tekchak mei*
*thanga upit aran mei*
*lam chen kachakpu mei*
*krambi mei pinauo*
*halna nadalremna*
*meiy ang khut a palna*
*meisut thakka thong*
*santhong meirly aida channa*
*krambi mei nijababu kubio*
*krambl palma pibuknung*
*harao mathoi tongbi-o*

After citing this hymn they worship their deity by offering rice and cloth. According to the tradition of Meitei society there are different types of fires. All the fires have different uses and consequently consider fire as a sacred God. As fire is very essential to the society the Meiteis preserve its traditional art of making and its uses in the settlement as well. The Meiteis assumed that fire is created by the god of goodness who looks after their health and spreads peace in the world. Thus the rituals — 'Meigi Tengtha' indicates the significance of the fire god. The Amaibas and the Amaibis used to offer this ritual while preparing the sacred fire at the time of ancestor-worship.

# 11
# Ancestor-Worship of Ningthouja Clan

Ningthouja clan is the founder of the seven clans of the Meiteis. They worship their ancestors on the 15th day of Inga (June-July). Their maiden deity is Pakhangba, the founder of Ningthouja dynasty. The offering items are water from Nungjeng pukhri, Leishang Flower (Seligendelia species), Thamna-Khenjong (lotus leaf), fire from two-fold of flames. Leikhamwai Napu Nashen (a small plant) is used for sprinkling water, chakthang dao (dao homed) is used as their Clan sword; red strip Sareng (a typical fish) used as their offering fish: Heiba fruit (ficus species) and Ching Enseen (a hilly plant) is used as firewood.[1]

1. N. Khelchandra, *Khunung Lichat Sazat*, 1967, p. 11.

In this Apokpa Khuramba (ancestor-worship), they use a number of incantations such as Anam Athou Laison, Naheiron, Yumdei naksen and Meigi tengtha. The following are the hymns of Anam Athou Laison[2] (See Appendix 6)

*Ong hei, onghei rajoi menga, yaiga, thoura rang, thourit thoudinglangbu, thourit thaba pongthou tamme. Thaba mabu laningle. Yawa konkhangsagi pongthou mathang pijage kumja palo thouge nongja palo thouganarenganlare terare oong ha oong hei ong hei.*

*Lahanong-nong mongba tudou khondou nong, tuting khongthon nongbu thourit thougarang thourit thoudin langbu, thourit thabapongthou tamme, thaba mabu lalnangdi, numit pongthou tamme, numit mabu lalangde, yawa kongthangshagi ponthou mathong pizage, kumja palli thonge, ngalareterare, oong hei onghei onghei.*

*Nahanong Tekpi moakcha, keirei mayancha, kowren masalcha, yanglei touba mahuicha, pongkhut kai sakaibana namlaba, laklababu phiji phina tonna humla latlababu thourit thouya rang thourit thoudinglangbu thourit thaba pongthou tamme, thaba mabu lalnangdi*

2. N. Khelchandra, Khunung Lichat Sazat, Pub. 1967, p. 21.

*numit pongthou tamme. Numit mabu lalnagdi. Yawa kongkhangsagi pongthou mathong pizage kunja palo thouge, nongja palo thouge, nganlari terari, oong hei, oong hei, oong hei, oong hei.*

# 12
# Pakhangba Chenghongba

A ritual known as pakhangba chenghongba is performed on the fifteenth day of the Month Kalen (April-May). In the book "Khunung Lichat Sajat", edited by Pandit Thongam Madhop Singh and N. Khelchandra, it is written as follows:

> *"Kalen thagi pankhat lakpa tara mangani*
> *panbada mabudhou pakhangba cheng honge.*
>
> *paonam hidendagi ikoukhatle chingu marambu*
> *khoiyam mamaibana sana lamok saktuna maba*
> *pena khongbana lai themgatlaga leima ningthou*
> *leipak myam phamdou ningthouna pukhatle.*
> *laisang youraga maibana anam athou kokle.*
> *nahei thoklaga ahonglon shak-i, penana phammang khalli.*
> *mabina chingu udaba mami tam khoiyum*

*khang daba mapa-laktuna laipao chelli*
*leipak myamna harao kummei touduna nungai mathoi*

***tonge, ngamjaba cheng chak, yensang napi thum nga***

*masing lakngamdana katlaga chakcha heijanaye".*

A translation of the above is as follows:

On the fifteenth day of the month of kalen (April-May) i.e. on full moon day a ritual known as "Pakhangba Chenghongba" is done from paonam hiddengi, a ghat of the course of the Imphal, river in the area of Kangla, the old capital of Manipur.

The maibas (priests) sing the song called 'sana lamok'. The maibas and pena khongbas (indigenous instrument players) perform lai themgatpa (calling out the spirit of the deity from water) and bring the spirit of the deity by the nobles, high officials known as phamdou ningthous. On reaching the temple, the maiba (priest) performs the ritual anam athou kokpa by citing the hymns call naheiron.

The maibi (priestess) performs leipao chenba (prediction).[1] The people in the locality offer rice and fresh items of vegetables to the deity. This particular

1. MS – Masil.

ritual function is nominally practised by traditional religious group at Sanamahi temple situated in the First Manipur Rifle Ground. The following are the different hymns used by the maibas in the rites of pakhangba chenghongba.

## SANA LAMOK

*Korou Ningthouren O*
*Lairen Wangba Meidingthou*
*Sana Namiren Miren Thouyangbabu*
*Yireklak Lamlellakki Kole.*

*Imu Igau Lengi*
*Tharei Lembi Lakki*
*Turel Kaosum Kaorangnungi*
*Taibang chingumang Khaigat Lakke*
*Punshi Nongshangna Sanamiren*
*Miren Thouyangbabu Tillaramale.*
*Sana Thongjinbu Ponna Lisillakle*
*Naraak Chinbu Kanna chongsinlakle,*
*Mi Kaplak Netharakle*
*Miyairen Kanna Chongna*
*Lairen sana Nathongjil*
*Thonglen Mongyambabu Kanna Chongna*
*Tubi Nachatlam Lairenna Fanshang*
*Thongnang Lallu Lisingsuna*

*Thonglen Tanmu Chanetlambu*
*Tubi Nachin Hen*
*Lairen Naroilangna Waionglak O*

*Malem mana Loi*
*Thabi Matang Ten*
*Yawa Sinthong Kham*
*Tarengkhongfang Leidana Mikoubadi*
*Tubi Nachin Hen*
*Lairen Narai Langhourakle*
*Lairen Nangbu*

*Fula Langna Thugamde*
*Fula Tongkhan lang*
*Lirentangma Langna Kapyolak Le.*

Sana Lam-ok is an old book. It is used during the time of worshipping of king Pakhangba, the historical king of Manipur. It is used by the Maibas (Priests) only and strict precautions are made before citing the hymns. To maintain it or to use it correctly, the Maibas used to get training from the experienced ones. In this regard an old saying is prevalents that any mistakes, while citing the rituals, considered harmful for the place. Sana Lam-ok is also a poem according to the local Pandits. It is also mentioned in connection with the coronation ceremony of the Meitei Kings. However, we could not trace and find as to who and when it was written (See Appendix 7). They, also, sing when they eulogise the glorious activities of the king.

### NAHEIROL

*Ha Ooing Hayeng, Thoubitang, Laibitang,*
*Chengleingaan, Tangleingaan Ungangei*
*Wagangei Sinsugei Sasugei Charoina*

*Khonglamgei Yambina Khoidamgei*
*Huithougei Chiphangei Keirenna*
*Yathokgei, langmaina Maihangei,*
*Langmai Hichin Hiyathama Thingaigei*
*Laokhaigei, Pureiromba Agak Agao Hau,*
*Sikak, sikai Haurababu manaiba Tampak*
*Leihaumai, Langmai Leihaumaibina Tairen*
*Longba Louna Laiza khikfen chairabada*
*Pureiromba Maron Thokle Mari Thokle*

*Khun Thanna, Laan Thana Kharou Lairou Koi,*
*Nongchup nongpok Koi Chupehi Laiji*
*Kanare Paanare Shengnarase,*
*Tin Leiragano Lai Leiragano.*

The ritual is offered to ward off the evil spirit that is believed to occupy the mind of the common people, the nobles and especially the Kings (See Apendix No. 8). It also indicates that people used to worship when the morning sun rose and fell on Langmaijing Ching (Hills) which is currently known as Baruni. During the reign of Chandrakriti Singh this particular hill was renamed as Baruni, which is a Hindu name. The long reign of this king produced an economic prosperity, religious zeal and enthusiasm.

After Naheiron the hymns of Ahonglon are as follows:

## AHONGLON[2]

*hehou hehou hehou*
*hongnemlo hongnemlo*
*hongnemse hongnemse*
*lamlenmadahongnemba*
*madaimadahongnemba*
*kangleiyonda hongnemba*
*pungmayondahongnemba*
*khoimathoubu hongnemba*
*laiyingthoubu hongnemba*
*lalreny aina nanongyaina hongnemba*
*liklirenna ningthourenna hongnemba*
*loidamgidi tha kaudana*
*langheigidi kum kaudana hongnemba*

2. MS-Ahonglon

*khoiy ampuga lalrampuga hongnemba*
*sanglengidi tengmalthinba, ahummakna khabigidi yoimloi houna*
*aseigidi khongphanglengna*
*kouba kana lakthong k ana*
*chinguwaina hongnemba*
*thongban wai na hongnemba*
*thongyigidi khongjromba masumakhang*
*shora wairou panba manasom*

The Ahonglon ritual indicated that the Meitei kings used to organise 'Ahong Kumei' — a grand feast along with song, dance and music. People from different Leikais (Locality) came with offerings and gathered at the palace. Their organisation and celebration on this occasion symbolise the memory of the deceased progenitors. Once in a year, after the advent of Vaishnavism, it was known as Kirtan (See Appendix 9).

# 13
# Koorak Lamtaiba

Koorak Lamtaiba is an annually performed rite and ritual of the Meitei. It is celebrated in the month of Inga (May-June). The objective of this ritual is to immolate the village deity to free the village cattle from the epidemic disease from insects and pest in the rice field and to avoid any sort of harm to the villagers from the evil spirits. The day after the performance of this rite and ritual the domesticated cattle are not allowed to get loose in and around the village. Every village has different forms of rites and rituals. Even among the Chakpa (a scheduled caste village) they have their separate rites and rituals in different ways. On the day itself the villagers are freed from their normal duties like cutting of firewood from the nearby hills and ploughing in the field. Moreover, the villagers do not move to far off places. On the other hand people coming from other villages are also not accepted and allowed to stay in the village. Even the outsider who stays in the village for certain purposes is also advised by the villagers to stay somewhere outside the village on this particular day. This rite and ritual is usually performed on a Namungba day of the month i.e. the eighth or twenty-third day of the month Inga (May-June).

On this specific day the village authority make a public avowal that the next day being of Koorak Lamtaiba, nobody would be allowed to move freely in the village. They should stay in their respective houses. They make some type of obstacles in the four village gates with the help of green branches of a free known as chang (a typical tree). In such situation if a person enters the village knowingly or unknowingly, the person is arrested by the village authority and brought to the village office. Then he is compelled to worship the village deity and has to offer fine (in cash or in kind) to the village deity. After fulfilling this action the offender is set free.

In chakpa phayeng (a scheduled caste village) on this particular day the rites and rituals are performed twice a day: one in the morning and the other in the evening. They have two sacred places. Luplakpa (local head) of the village leads the morning ceremonial functions and the other ceremony is led by Khullakpa (head of the village). One-day prior to this day the village authority makes a public announcement that nobody is allowed to move freely in the village on this particular day. Even the participants of ceremonial function, also, will have to stay in the village office until the evening ceremony is over. The following hymns are rendered:

> *"yammalai sawangga yathang y amma lai sly angga thang, yeptre yeptre"*

The village chief or chieftain renders this hymn. It is known as Yeptre Loaba. Then the four persons among the participants go around the village by holding spears and shields in their hands. If anybody is found violating the restrictions given here they are arrested. This is known as Ketloi Koiba. The arrested persons are required to worship the village deity and after giving advice by the village elders they are released. In the evening the participants from the village office beat the big village drum. It signifies an announcement for the commencement of the evening ceremony. Then the village Longloi (officials) come to the sacred place to perform the rites and rituals.

Another official rank-holders known as Singthapham do not join the evening ceremony.

Generally, in the morning, some village youth go out to the field for catching Kaujeng (grasshopper) with the help of a net. This practice is known as Kaojeng Haiba. In the morning Kaojengs are offered to the village deity. The offerings i.e. kaojeng are fried and made singju (Salad). It is one of the indigenous items for their dish. Other important items for offering are egg (duck), a black coloured dog and one hen. Each village has different offering items. In some villages they offer pigeons whereas other villages offer hen and pork.

# 14
# The Role of Male and Female in the Ritual Process

In the olden days the Meiteis believed in God very strongly. They believed that God is all in all and that the results of whatever they did were in the hands of the Creator. And so, they were interested in prayers and offerings to Gods and Goddesses. They believed that any natural calamity like burning of houses, epidemic etc. were caused by Gods and Goddesses in order to punish human beings for their ill behaviour. In such cases Amaibis and Amaibas, hand-in-hand, performed their public duties as priestesses and priests by way of the prayers and offerings. It is a believed that Amaibis and Amaibas were endowed with supernatural powers for knowing, by way of asking their respective spirits, the causes of such calamities and the means for mitigation of the same by prayers and offerigs.

So, in this context, if we have to investigate the role of males and females in the ritual process, we have to start from the role of Amaibas and Amaibis. However, it is better to first have a clear idea of what Amaibi is. In my interview with certain persons ranging from a layman to an academician, "Amaibi" is described as the person who can tell or foretell the fate of a person with supernatural powers. Prominent Amaibis and local pandits in different parts of Manipur are of the same opinion. Amaibi can also be considered as an equal term the 'Shaman'. Hersbouits opined that the Shaman is an individual endowed with supernatural powers to hear, or one who can call his spirit to find out what is beyond time and space.

'Amaibi' is, sometimes, also called 'Maibi'. The term Maibi is feminine. Some people take these two terms as different ones. They distinguish Amaibis as those persons who perform the functions relating to Gods and Goddesses. Such an 'Amaibi' known as 'Khamnung Changba' (who performs divination). And Maibis are those who perform midwifery functions. Such a midwife Maibi is described as Khamnung Changba (who does not perform divination). However, now-a-days, it is generally thought better to use only one term as 'Maibi' although their functions are of different kinds. It is also to be noted that there is no sexual bar for becoming an Amaibi. Both sexes, male and female, can become an Amaib, although, most of the Amaibis are female.

There is a clear functional relation between Amaiba, the priest and Amaibi, the priestess. Amaibas are those menfolk who perform religious functions with or without the assistance of an Amaibi. There is also a clear distinction between 'Amaibi and Amaiba'. Amaibas are those men who perform religious functions and Maibas are those who perform medical treatments for curing disease and perform certain rites for the dead. In the modern usage the Maibas are known as "Beita" (Beidya).

There is a close relation between Amaiba and Amaibi. They cannot discard each other. Both are essential for performing a rite. However an Amaiba or an Amaibi can perform a rite by only himself or herself, if the help is a minor one. But, major public rites and rituals such as "Lai Haraaoba" can only be performed by the coordination of Amaibas and Amaibis.

The importance of both Amaiba and Amaibi can be inferred for the performance of several traditional rites like, 'Kurak Lamdaiba', 'Kongba Leithong Phatpa', 'Cheiraoba', 'Yaosang', etc. However in the 'Saroi Khangba' the ritual is performed by Amaibis only.

## BECOMING OF AN AMAIBI

In the olden days only incarnated women became Amaibis. But now-a-days, as population increases day by day, only those women who possess supernatural powers become Amaibis. Every person cannot become an Amaibi. A woman who would became an Amaibi can be distinguished from the rest by observing her habits in respect of eating, movements etc. For example, these women do not like to eat the Ngakra fish. The eating is usually followed by vomiting tendency. A would-be Amaibi knows her right mother "Guru". When the would-be Amaibi becomes frenzied with obsession, she cannot be controlled by any Amaibi Guru but by her 'right Amaibi Guru' only. The would-be Amaibi in her frenzy always tries to run like a mad girl to her right of 'Mother Guru' even at the sight of hers.

## LIFE-WAYS OF AMAIBI

The life of Amaibi is not a simple and ordinary one. It is somewhat complex and arduous in nature, as they have to maintain a way of life moulded and shaped as to fit in the spiritual world. From the very beginning to the end of their life, they observe a number of rules. As a result of the strict observances of the intricate rules they, as they think, possess their spiritual power of having communion with Gods and Goddesses. When they become too old and weak to maintain the strict ways of life and perform religious functions, they give up the spiritual life and follow an ordinary human life.

Any person who is going to be an Amaibi in future must have spiritual powers by birth. In Manipur no father or mother wants their daughter to become an Amaibi and so, even though they know their child cannot be checked from becoming an Amaibi, they try their level best to suppress the inherent supernatural powers of their child, as a result of which a child sometimes faces unnatural death.

Besides the role of Amaibas and Amaibis, in the Meitei society, there is no restriction for the participation of womenfolk and menfolk in the religious ceremonies. Manipuri women, mainly in the valley, are governed by the norms and practices prescribed by both Meiteism, the old religion of the Meiteis and Hinduism. The same can be said in the case of women in the hill areas of Manipur. Women in the hills are governed by their indigenous social norms as well as the norms prescribed by Christianity. Women perform pujah, learn Mantras, go to pilgrimage, etc. This fact is amply illustrated in the Lai Haraoba festival where women perform dance and songs. Lai

Haraoba means 'pleasing of Gods'. The essence of the festival is to please the Lais (Gods) in order to gain their favour. In this regard, E. Nillakanta expressed his view that 'Lai Haraoba' mirrors the entire culture of Manipuri people. It reveals its strengths and weaknesses, the beliefs and superstitions and perhaps charm and happiness of the Manipuri people.

It may be noted that changes came after the coming of Hindu Vaishnavism in Manipur. The priests started to take major role in the performance of the religious ceremonies. These changes affected the position of the Maibis. But the changes could not eliminate the importance of Maibis from the Manipuri society especially the Meitei society. Manipuri women especially Meitei women participated actively in the Hindu-oriented festivals like Yaosang (Doljatra or Holi), Rathajatra, Durga Puja, Jhulan etc. Though these are Hindu festivals, they are normally observed in a traditional way of the Manipuris in the society.

Vaishnavism, which became a state religion about two hundred years ago during the reign of Garibniwaz could not suppress the public prominence of women in major ritual performances despite its patriarchal ideology. Then the Brahmin families, which were the agents of spreading Sanskritic ideology to the people, worship Sanamahi and Leimarel, the traditional presiding deities of the Meitei household. Moreover, the Brahmins go to a Maibi when they need her ritual services. The new faith has thus adapted to the local religious environment forming a distinct identity of its own, different from the pan-Indian Hinduism, which has its root in the patriarchal mainstream culture of India.

Apart from Amaiba and Amaibi, a common man and woman of Meitei society, also, normally performs the ritual service to the deities. Every Vaishnavite Meitei family has a sacred religious place locally known as Tulsibong, where a basil plant is planted on an earthen mound in its courtyard. This place is cleaned by a woman of the family every morning and morning prayer is performed by a woman after purifying herself ritually by taking a bath. However, a girl, who has not attained puberty, can perform the prayer without taking a bath. Thus, a bath brings a change in the ritual status of both man and woman. There is certain social restriction defining her social jurisdiction.

- Women are not allowed to eat the things, which was offered to family God at the time of Apokpa Khurumba (Ancestor-Worship).

- There is a saying 'Nupina Luhongpham Anirak Phamheide' which means women cannot sit on the wedding seat twice.

- A woman cannot cook without taking a bath because cooking itself is regarded as a sacred act.
- A woman suffering from pollution during her menstrual period and the period of three months after child delivery is not allowed to lead a normal life. She is prevented from participating in religious activities, the domain of the sacred world.
- A woman who suffers from menstrual pollution can regain the state of purity by taking a bath. However, a purificatery rite has to be performed by a Brahmin priest for the restoration of the normal condition of the woman, who is being considered polluted because of childbirth.

Thus, in Meitei society women do not suffer from any religious disability. They equally share with men in the performance of almost all the religious activities. For instance, in Rasalila and Sankirtana, the major religious rituals of Vaishnavism, the participation of women shows the importance of women in the Vaishnavite religious world. Sankirtana is performed by women only at the royal temple. The women participants dance around the images of Radha and

Krishna kept at the centre of the arena taking the role of Gopis. In this dance, of which the performance is regarded as the special privilege of women. They are joined by male participants, drummers and musicians.

# 15
# Changing Trends in the Ritual Life of the Meiteis

In traditional background, ritual is the strongest element and it still exerts some influence on the Meiteis of Manipur. The term 'ritual' involves belief in religious power and, therefore, is sacred. Ritual symbolises the integrating force. It is something shared by the whole community or at least by a section of it. Rituals determine the social content and behaviour of a group. They may also reflect the changing aspects of society. Such changing aspects may signify the creation of a new aspect in the form of a new tradition or redefinition of an old one.

Today, in the Meitei society of Manipur, the ritual ceremony is a blend of traditional Meitei and that of mainland India. It is meant to say that they used to observe both the pure traditional Meitei rituals and Meitei Hindu rituals. For decades, these two blendings have been inseparable and have become an integrating force between different sections of Manipuri society.

Many eminent scholars and researchers propagate that in the area of rites and the rituals, the Vaishnav Hinduism influence is great. Hinduism succeeded in diluting, and sometimes, even disintegrating, the rites and rituals pertaining to the traditional Meitei faith. A few new Hindu rites and rituals were also adopted and incorporated. All the other intermediate rites of passages were influenced by Hinduism, which nevertheless retained some of the traditional cultural characteristics with new elements incorporated and old elements modified, the rites and rituals pertaining to this society, evolved as 'Meitei Hindu Rituals', rather than just as Hindu rituals. Every human society, nonetheless and the Meitei society, undergoes changes in the process of response to many types of changes whether man-made or natural which are sometimes beyond human control. The emergence of the Meitei society into the modern era may be said to have started since the beginning of the present century as a result of two main forces which caused a change in their world-view and provided the spring-board for changes in different fields. The two forces are modernisation and Westernisation. Other forces are subsidiary to them. The people of the valley were proud to be Hindus and could legitimately boast of their artistic expression which won increasing recognition not only in India but also abroad.

## REVIVALIST SPIRIT

A wave of revivalist movement upstaged which had its origin in the '30s. A large number of people-academician, social activists, and even the common people assume it as Meitei Renaissance or Renaissance in Manipur. A Manipuri scholar has singled out two persons viz. Naoria Phulo (from Cachar of Assam) and Uyam Irabot who initiated the new movement, to the utter neglect of socio-political movements and literary awakening in the early part of twentieth century in Manipur. Naoria Phulo started Apokpa Marup with its accent on old Manipuri gods and goddesses like Sanamahi and Pakhangba. It was a reaction of Vaishnavism and had an ethnic dimension, as Sanskrit was totally replaced by chaste Manipuri expression. This happened in the form of protest and reached the valley soon and minority movement sprang up. It found a positive echo in the minds of the young people in their search for ethnic identity and affected the creative expression of young writers and scholars of

Manipur to a considerable extent. This renaissance in Manipur was not likely to go along a steady and clean path. There has practically been no path. However, with the expansion of English education i.e. higher education or mass education in the 1940s, the renaissance became multi-pronged and multi-layered affair and it affected the community at various levels. Consequently, the image of this movement has had a great impact on a section of Meitei community especially the lower middle class people. The change that emanate from this impact is witnessed from the early '80s. In the realm of rites and rituals, the calendaric ritual activities, which had not been performed for years, started being remembered and well revered. But the concept that every culture is different and distinct prevailed. This is true in matters of rituals and ceremonies also. But not withstanding these outer differences, every culture and its religion flows from the same fundamental source, the Creator. Since the deeper spiritual truth is fundamentally the same everywhere, it is not easily comprehensible by the majority. It is, therefore, common in every culture to weave its rites and rituals, tales and folklores to symbolise and express them. In this view scholars, pandits, and intelligentsia of that time, and even of present times, tried and are still trying to draw a parallel between Hindu and Meitei gods and to the extent that they attempted to derive an evolutionary line from Indra that for some Atiya Sidaba became Brahmin Gotras and Vishnu became the ancestor of all royal descendants, replacing Pakhangba. Nongpok Ningthou became Shiva.

## THE CHANGING TREND

There is no denying the fact that old ritual values have considerably been lost. Economic motives have become important factors now-a-days and rituals like Lai Keithel Kaba, Pakhangba chenghongba and Kurak Lamtaiba are becoming rare. People simply cannot afford to perform them. This is meant to say that by minimising the original form of the rituals. They are performed nominally. But not in the form of deviation. The lengthy process is shortened to save energy, time and space. However, the lyrics in the hymns of the ritual are properly preserved. Any form of duration is checked by the Pandit Loishang or Maiba Loishang, a department of royal scholars and priests. This department currently exists and its office is situated in the palace compound. The problem is that since the hymns are written in archaic Manipuri language the people understanding them are becoming less and less who understand and can cite the rituals. Due to the influence of modern education such language becomes less important and almost antiquated. Moreover those prominent scholars who mastered in this language and rituals are very few; and many of them at present are very weak and ageing.

As also mentioned above in the '80s and in the early '90s the ritual life of the Meiteis have gone through some change. For instance in pertaining to the festival of Yaosang (Holi) which lasted for five days has been converted into Yaosang sport. After the local Brahmin had performed the Puja and recited devotional songs (Kirtan) praising Lord Krishna, the image is then taken out and the hut is burnt which indicates the beginning of the festival. In the very next day i.e. from the second day children indulge in different items of sports. Boys and girls in small group going from door to door asking for donation has largely declined. The game of smearing colour on the face and sprinkling water during the festival, which is known as Pichakari is hardly seen. Yet on the whole, people play for a while with the mood of the festival. The elders, however, celebrate in a more formal and devotional manner. They go to the Sri Gobindajee temple located in the palace ground area. Groups of singers singing devotional songs congregate here and enter the dance arena to get themselves wet with colours sprinkled on them by the Brahmin priests. They all the time sing Bhajans and addressing each other with 'Hari Bol' (Say Hari) and 'He Hari' (Hail Hari). The woman dressed as Gopis then dance in the style of the 'Raas Lila' with colourful sticks in their hands. Getting beaten by them is considered a good fortune. The essence of 'Yaosang' seems to lie here. But, the new generation seems to have diverted and put emphasis on sport and consider the particular festival as sports festival. However, 'Thabal Chongba', one of the oldest forms of folkdance, is strictly preserved. All the youths consider that without Thabal Chongba the Yaosang festival is meaningless.

In my interview with some of the local clubs, which organised sports, revealed that the emergence of the sports-meet will curb the youths from unwanted behaviours. Moreover it aims at bringing out young talent in the field of sports. In fact it is to encourage sports in the society. Some others opined that the duration of the festivals is very long and consequently affects the economy. At present the first three days are purely observed and the remaining are diverted to other activities like sports and other competitions for children. Due to this changing trends the present generation is ignorant of the symbolic representation of 'Yaosang' (Holi) festival and its ritualistic significance. In short, the mind of the youths are preoccupied by Yaosang Sports.

In regard to Cheiraoba, at present, there are two types-one is Mayang Cheiraoba and the other is Meitei Cheiraoba. Earlier the Meitei followed the former one, which was considered to be influenced by Vaishnavism. All the Hindu Manipuris celebrate this festival on the last day of the year, and this day comes off on the last day of Chaitra month of the Bengali Calendar. Later, in the early 80s, a revivalist group called Meitei Marup started organising Meitei Cheiraoba. Though, in the beginning, the Meitei Cheiraoba could not get much response, yet with the influence of tradition it has started gaining grounds. In the present day, a large section of the Meiteis celebrated Meitei Cheiraoba festivals with the notion that they have separate 'New Year' day and do not correspond to that calendar of Vaishnavism. The Meitei Brahmins and other Meitei Hindus follow the Mayang Cheiraoba and celebrate the ritual festivals strictly even today. The difference that one can witness between the two is that in Meitei Cheiraoba people can have fish items in the feast. But in the Mayang Cheiraoba only pure vegetables are allowed. However, the rituals are more or less the same and indiscriminately the entire society in the valley enjoys both the festivals. The State Government also declares holidays on both the occasions.

Another current trend in the ritual life of the Meiteis is Ancestor-Worship (Apokpa Khurumba). This is meant to say that people are becoming more conscious of their Origin, Genealogy, Identity, History and Kinship. From the sociological point of view the Ancestor-Worship creates mutual understanding between clan members; enables to communicate and bring closer the clan members who have settled in different parts of the society. Secondly, it strengthens the institution of family, marriages and kinship system. In my fieldwork, the Ancestor-Worship – now-a-days, is found mainly organised by the Sageis (sub clan). This indicates that the gathering started from the micro level to macro level. And a big political ideology is associated with it. The message of this ritual function is propagated through media with a common title "Sagei Paogel" (News of subclan gathering). Consequently, from the socio-political point of view, we can conclude that this particular ceremony takes a great role in bringing identity formation and subjective self-consciousness.

## THE RITUAL LIFE OF CURRENT GENERATION

A snap survey of a small section of the youth, conducted, underscores the trend. Only sixteen per cent, when asked if they were religious, said no. Eighty four percent said they sought solace in religion. And fifty-four per cent said they often visited a place of worship. In fact, education in social sciences was modelled on the western value system — rationality, objectivity, scrutiny, and secularity. The secular understanding of religion is that it is basically a human creation. From this secular point of view the majority of students support the secular and argue that there is a god.

But, in the survey of exploratory research design the current generation of youngsters has not properly realised the depth of their own ancient culture. There is a growing desire among the youth to understand their own culture and religion; but under the influence of nationalism and sub-nationalism they are caught between two thoughts. One is the traditional Meitei religion and the other of Mainland India i.e. Hinduism. Our research findings reveal out that due to the consciousness of their history and identity, the old way of worship continues-they worship Soraren, Pakhangba, Sanamahi, Ima Leimarel and 363 Umanglais (Local deities) scattered in all parts of Manipur. A religious syncretism occurred and a fine synthesis had been affected. At the same time, the indigenous Meitei gods and goddesses were identified with that of the Hindu Pantheon. Thus Soraren, King of Heaven, was identified with Indra, Nongpok Ningthou with Shiva, Panthoibi with Durga or Parvati, Wangbaren, the water god with Varuna, etc. In the religious festivals of these gods and goddesses the rituals are not deviated, they are strictly preserved. However, the Amaiba and Amaibis, the royal scholars and local Pandits who can cite and know the rituals are diminishing day by day. On the other hand, the young generation possess minimum tendency to learn the in-depth knowledge of the rituals which is written in archaic Manipuri language. The values of the rituals are diminishing and only the festivities are increasing. Their knowledge is believed to be at the superficial level and their attitude is influenced by various political mechanisms.

# Appendix 1
# Incantation

The incantation is written in archaic Manipuri language praising the ten deities or sovereign gods and also known as Ningthou Pongba Tara (Ten Kings) who guards different directions of the Manipur. We have translated only the first three Paras because the remaining are the same.

Hey Lord Koubru also known as Kaubaren and his daughters — Kounu Leimacha and Leimacha Kakyai who settled and roamed in different hill ranges. The fifteen hill ranges were also occupied by 'Lai' group of people; where flora and fauna are abundantly available; summer and winter regularly arrive in time; and have very fertile ranges with abundantly well grown fruitful trees. Please give us these entire well-being and the prosperity You possess.

Hey Lord Thongnang and your surrounding hills, covered by Koubru's hill ranges. The beautiful place where the Khaba's took shelter, and facing towards the east direction. Please also give Your prosperities and also make us like them.

Hey Lord Ipu Hangoi Ningthou Atiya Sidaba, also known as Lord Maharava. You are the creator of the Universe. You are the creator of day and night. You are the creator of all the living and none living beings, and also you are the Ordained. Your backbone is the main pillar; your belly is the sky. Your words and power give ten months of conception period for human beings, Samok (Swine), Sagol (Horse) and Sandang (Like Ox); five months for Hameng (Goat) and Oak (Swine/Pig); One month for Hui (Dog), Khunu (Pigeon) and Nganu (Duck). Please give to us also the power You have. Give us Your prosperity and lead us to a peaceful life.

# Appendix 2
# Apoklon

The Amaibis (Priestess) perform the rituals of Apoklon to invoke the almighty creator Gods-the creator of Universe, the creator of seven salais in the valley and the hills and also others. It includes the creator God of all the herbs like charot, Phaiang, Taumu, etc. of the valley: the creator of fungus plants like Chengum (Mushroom), Uyen (Lintinellus), Uchena (Hirola auricula), Tektekpal, yenkhurai, etc.: the creator of rooted plants like the kaukha, ...... etc.

The creator of big trees from which boat of the kings can be made: the creator of all the birds; the creator of all the fruit bearing trees; the creator of all the bamboo trees; creator of all the rice of different species grown in the hills and the valley; creator of different species of fish including all the creatures of water; the creator of all the domestic and wild animals; the creator of all the different species of insects like flies, leeches, ants, bees, etc.

# Appendix 3
# Declaration of the Outgoing Cheithaba

My master and Lord, Thou art the God king, the brave great sky, the God of man, the leader of men. May the queen and the king live long with prosperity, abundant rice, fish, wealth and salt in this year of my friend who hasn't taken all the evils onto his shoulder, more than the last year for which I shouldered.

# Appendix 4
# Declaration of the Incoming Cheithaba

My master and Lord, Thou art the God king, the brave great sky, the God of man, the foremost of man. The years of the two great kings, Pakhangba and Jainou, Chingshomba, the king of Langmais were celebrated in continuity as the fire burnt and the phalangs of the body joined with Kongba Leithong Phatpa, Sajibu Leikhun Phunba (opening of soil at Kongba and closing of it in Sajibu) during the reign of each king continually. The stick of the Khok bamboo which was used to control or put-off the wild fire, attack in war by the warrior, make handles for dows, spears etc. and with two branches at the end, was collected and a bell was attached on it and thus Cheithaba was celebrated heralding the coming of a new year, with the Khok sticks on their shoulders and the clank of the bells, travelling through the streets and the lanes. Let all the evils, the news of war and the wild beasts and all the enemies of the coming year fall into Tharei and Lemlei. I take upon my shoulder all diseases, useless messages of war, collusions and conflicts to carry away with me. My Lord and master, Thou art the God king, the brave great Sky. May thou be granted with prosperity, a populous and abundant country of the great breadth and the length as the new year sets in.

# Appendix 5
# Meigi Tengtha

Fire burnt with bright flame
Fire burnt with low flame
Fire burnt from rubbing two stones
Fire burnt from Kambi (a trail oval small pot used for worshipping deities)
Fire burnt from Khoijum Leikham plant (a Meitei traditional plant)
Fire burnt for brewing wine.

Fire burns from colliding two thang (dao)
Fire burns by striking iron on stone
Fire burns in the wood forest
Fire burns and preserve in the earthen pot
Fire burns to light the room or any place
Fire burns in the hill areas
Fire converts from small flame to big one
Fire shared by the local people for various purposes
Fire brought by Poireiton and used in Establishing Village

Fire used in worshipping Goddess Ayangleima
Fire burnt for cultivation
Fire burnt by youth for making bonfire

Fire burnt at the time of women of the Chakpas
Fire burnt for making pot
Fire kept on potsherds
Fire burnt from thatch
Fires that bum and produce thick smoke

Fire burns in the field of Hao (Tribal) areas
Fire burns at a place called Thanga
Fires that fly and burn
With the faggot on the fire
In the direction of South West
We beg You to give all the fires
We pray to You heartily

We request You to make us happy and let the fires burn wide.

# Appendix 6
# Sana Lamok

King who came from heaven
King who came from heaven
King who came from heaven
King greater than all the almighty Gods
Your quality and power give water to the valley.

River runs from Arong to Sugnu
And from the South of Sugnu to others
You came floating through rice fields, forests, dead lands
And gathered with us showing your full might and kindness

You approached the Gate of Kangla
You bravely entered deflating many enemies
You broke many barriers

You beheaded many opponents
Then you became the king and owner of the place.

You protect yourself from the revolt
From interference in your work
At last you abolished all the difficulties
And became the king.

# Appendix 7
# Anam Athou Laison

Oh! Lord
Thou the creator of the world
Thou the creator of the terrestrial
Thou got the power of supernatural
Please open your door
We perform our duties in your creation
Thou create day and night
In it we all are living
Your spirit create the universe
In your creation we are dwelling
And follow your movement
Your movements and changes are never ending.

All human being, from the beginning, construct their fathom and canal for their survival.

This activity is also included in your journey.

The mistake we commit in your creation drag us down in a dark dungeon.

The moment we remind you and pray you to release us from the darkness.

You love us at that very moment.

In your creation we are always contended; also sometimes deviated.

But, everything happens in day and night of yours.

You are omnipresent, you have seen everything.

Even though we make offence, you forgive. Your kindness guides us.

Let us also take part and settle in your creation.

Oh God the creator of the world

Inside your creation.

We all are praying citing your name.

# Appendix 8
# Naheirol

When the morning comes up

And the Sun shines

All the Creatures—animals, birds and human beings have started their own duties.

When Sun rays falls on the face of Langmaiging ching, the settlers spell out and utter the name of the almighty god

At the same time Amaiba (Priest) and Amaibis (Priestess) also perform their duties

They nourish all the people affected by evil spirit

They ward off the evils from Pureiromba a renowned person of the Khuman; Sprinkling holy water by using toon leafs. He regains from his numbness.

Then, they pray to the evil spirit to compromise from afflicting each other.

# Appendix 9
# Ahonglon

Hey Hou Hey Hou Hey Hou
People rise
Let us celebrate
Let us celebrate
To a particular place
At the centre of Kangleipak
Under the jurisdiction of the palace
Let the Lai (God) and King celebrate
Let their son and grandson also celebrate
Let the great king celebrate festivals

For every year, every season and every month
Let forefather of Lai group of people
And forefather of Me group of people
Together celebrate happiness
Let the nobles also gather

With the Amaibi, Pena player, folk singer and others

The 'Me' group sit on northern side

With the Lai group celebrate festivals

Eatables are distributed

Grand feast organised

Lord Thangiji Khongchromba, the glorious king started the celebration.

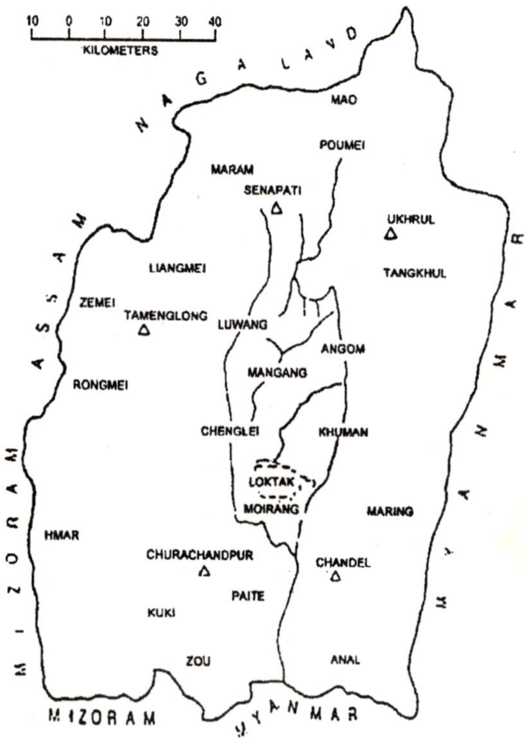


**Map:** Clan Principalities with Other Ethnic Communities Dispersed in the Region of Manipur

# Index


Ahong Khamsa, 48-9
Ahonglon ritual, 81
Amaibas, 70, 87, 89, 93, 107
Amaibi Guru, 90
Anantasai, king, 41
Ancestor-worship, 45-6, 49-51, 64-5, 67, 70, 72, 93, 105
  Khaba Nganba Clan, 67
  Khuman Clan, 63
  Moirang Clan, 45
  Ningthouja Clan, 71
Ancient Meitei texts, 6, 53
Angoms, 43, 46, 49
Apoklon, 50, 57, 111
Apokpa Khuramba, 46, 50, 64, 67, 72, 93, 105
Archaic Manipuri language, 109

Bamboo, 55
Baruni, 80
Beliefs, 92, 97
Bengali literature and Manipuri literature, 18
Bishnupriya community, 9, 12
Boat race, 23
Brahmin priests, 94, 102
Brahmins, 93, 104

Calendaric rituals, 10, 100
Ceremonial function, 85
Ceremonial practice, 6
Chaitanya Vaishnavism, 8, 12
Christianity, 8, 91
Communion, 5, 91
Community movements, 9
Coronation ceremonies, 78
Cultivation, 23

Dao, 50, 67, 71, 115
Deities, 5, 28-30, 42, 50, 54-7, 61-2, 69, 76, 93, 109
  domestic, 59
  household, 60
  maiden, 63, 67, 71
  male, 42
  worshipping, 115

Divination, 88
Dominant group, 8

Earthen jars, 55-6
Ethnic community, 49
Ethnic group, 8
Evening ceremony, 85
Evil deities, 20
Evil spirit, 5, 61, 64, 79, 121

Female deities, 29, 42-3
Festival
  cheiraoba, 59, 104
  fertility, 38
  great king celebrate, 122
  Lai Keithel Kaba, 41-2, 44, 101
  religious, 37, 107
  sports, 103
  spring, 37
  Yaosang, 40, 102-3
Ficus species, 50, 63, 67, 71
Firewood, 46, 50, 55, 63, 67, 71, 83
Forest goddess, 61

Halangkar festival, 41
Harvest, 23, 31, 38
Heiba fruit, 50, 63, 67, 71
Hinduism, 8, 12, 38, 91, 98, 106
Hiyanggei, 21, 23
Holi, 37-9, 92, 102-3

Imphal valley, 48

Khaba Nganba, 49-50, 67
Khamnung Changba, 88
Kingship system, 8
Kongba, 48, 53, 113
Kongba river, 49, 54
Koorak Lamtaiba, 83-4

Lai group, 122
Langthrei – medicinal plant, 55-6
Leimaren, Goddess, 21
Leishang flower, 50, 63, 67, 71
Leithong Phatpa, 53
Loktak lake, 46-7, 50

Maiba Loishang, 101
Manipur valley, 17
Manipuri calendar, 16
Mayang Cheiraoba, 104
Medicinal plant, 55
Meitei calendar year, 27
Meiteism, 91
Misfortunes, 5, 54, 60
Morning ceremonial function, 84
Mythical King *see* Pakhangba

Naoria Phulo, 99
Ningthou, Goddess Nongpok, 38
Ningthouja, 46, 48

Old ritual values, 101
Orchid, 55

Paddy, 23, 54-5

Pakhangba, 40, 42, 49-50, 71, 78, 99, 106, 113
Ploughing, 22, 83
Presiding deities, 28

Religious activities, 94
Religious rituals, 15
Renaissance, 99-100
Revivalist group, 104
Rice, 23, 29, 39, 43, 55, 60, 76, 111-12
Rifle Ground, 77
Rites
  intermediate, 98
  purificatery, 94
  traditional, 89
Ritual ceremony, 97
Ritual festivals, 104
Royal maiba, 29

Salt cakes, 55
Seligendelia species, 50, 63, 67, 71
Sharoi Khangba, 27-30
Shree Shree Bijoygovinda temple, 41
Social functions, 6
Spiritual life, 91
Spiritual truth, 100
Supernatural powers, 87-8, 90-1

Tei Kings, 35
Thabal Chongba, 39, 103

Vaishnavism, 8, 11-12, 81, 92, 94, 99, 104
Village cattle, 83
Village deity, 83-6
Village drum, 85

Wakching, 21, 23
Water clock, 29
Yaosang, 37, 39-40, 89, 92, 102-3
  *see also* Holi
Yumjao lairemma, goddess, 28